NEW DIMENSIONS IN LITERATURE

INTRODUCTION
TO POETRY

Edgar H. Knapp

McCORMICK-MATHERS PUBLISHING COMPANY
Florence, Kentucky 41042

McCORMICK-MATHERS PUBLISHING COMPANY

New York   **Florence, Kentucky**

ii

CONTENTS

ix

xi

THE CLIMATE OF POETRY

Poetry is like climate. The climate of a place is the year-long average of individual moments of weather—involving unique combinations of temperature, air pressure, rainfall, humidity, cloud composition, and wind. Similarly, poetry as a type of literature is a composite of individual poems—involving unique combinations of grammar, sound, rhythm, thought, feeling, and appeals to the imagination. More profitable than defining poetry, perhaps, is the defining of a poem. A poem is an arrangement of words creating a moment of experience, like a batch of weather calculated to warm or chill us.

The stuff of poetry is the experience of this world, but experience of the world is not poetry until its substance has been reshaped in the workshop of the poet's imagination. Human experience is essentially a response to our environment. Moving through the weathers of our world, we develop feelings and attitudes, hopes and fears, which are our own internal weather. Robert Frost in his poem "Tree at My Window" (page 158) wisely refers to "inner and outer weather." The goal of the poet is to suggest human weathers as vividly and as freshly as possible, and the chief means is appeal to the readers' senses. The facts and figures of a weather report are tame knowledge in contrast to our sensations in a driving blizzard or on a warm day in April.

A memorable poem, like memorable weather, depends upon contrast for its effect. Sunlight is brighter for the presence of shadow. When the rain drums upon the drought-hard ground, we awake to a pattern in nature. So does contrast

1

give life to a poem. Poems in this book dramatize contrasts between loneliness and companionship, desire and duty, and what things appear to be and what they really are. These are the weathers of poetry, and they are the weathers of life.

Reading Poems Besides introducing you to good poems, this book will help you develop skills and attitudes which, it is hoped, will further your understanding and appreciation of poetry. The ways are frequently difficult. A poem is a combination of sound, sense, and feeling, and we rarely get the full effect of the combination all at once. We must be alert to the sense and suggestions which a poem makes, and with every additional reading we may find things we did not realize were there before.

The sense of a poem becomes clear with our understanding of the speaker, the meanings of words, the grammar and punctuation, and the organization of the total composition. A poem makes its suggestions through the actual sounds and the rhythm of its language, as well as through its appeal to our senses. Rather than describing a feeling, then, a good poem evokes it.

After each of the poems in the pages ahead are questions and comments designed to help you "experience" the poem.

Imagery, Simile, and Metaphor Two techniques by which poets evoke feeling are *imagery* and *metaphor*. Imagery is the use of words which create a sense impression, such as seeing, hearing, or touching. "Bird songs pound the hollow vastness of the sky" is an auditory image. "White flower-tufts, thick on the branch" is a visual image. Metaphor is the combination of two essentially different images: "Bird songs pound the kettledrum sky" (*drum* and *sky* are discrete images), or "The pear tree, its arms braceleted with flowers" (*arms* and *branches*, *bracelets* and *flowers* are the essentially different elements). Complex imagery of this nature gives the poet a further dimension of expressiveness. Jean Starr Untermeyer's "High Tide" (page 12) owes much of its suggestive power to the combined images of wave action and ferocious hounds.

Metaphor has been defined more narrowly as "implied comparison." "The moon is a cookie" *implies* likeness or similarity, whereas "the moon is like a cookie" states the similarity. A second term—*simile*—then becomes necessary for a stated comparison in which *like* or *as* is used. An example of simile occurs on page 30, where W. D. Snodgrass says a slow-moving lobster on ice is "like a run down toy."

Nevertheless, during this sojourn into the climate of poetry, metaphor is defined broadly: the use of one thing to explain or illuminate another thing. Holding to the single term *metaphor* for comparisons both stated and implied will make your way less cluttered and highlight the common essence which they share.

Looking Ahead Questions and comments which follow the individual selections in the book are designed to aid your discoveries in the "climate" of poetry. Your alertness to the interplay of outer and inner weather will help you. Then, when you have adjusted the sights of your imagination, you will find the climate of poetry both relaxing and bracing.

RHYTHMS IN NATURE

Throughout the years one of the most popular subjects for poems has been the natural world. Perhaps the first green shoots changing to dark foliage and eventually blushing in their autumn decline have spoken to human beings of their own life cycle. The ten poems in this section depict scenes in a segment of nature's twelve-month cycle—from early spring to the onset of winter's frost.

One word of caution—your standards for judging these pictures should be different from those which you bring to a photograph. While both camera and poet do produce pictures of the world, only the camera records full visual detail. The poet selects details and images which will create a unified pattern of feeling.

KYOTO: MARCH

A few light flakes of snow
Fall in the feeble sun;
Birds sing in the cold,

A warbler by the wall. The plum
Buds tight and chill soon bloom.   5
The moon begins first
Fourth, a faint slice west
At nightfall. Jupiter half-way
High at the end of night-
Meditation. The dove cry   10
Twangs like a bow.
At dawn Mt. Hiei dusted white
On top; in the clear air
Folds of all the gullied green
Hills around the town are sharp,   15
Breath stings. Beneath the roofs
Of frosty houses
Lovers part, from tangle warm
Of gentle bodies under quilt
And crack the icy water to the face   20
And wake and feed the children
And grandchildren that they love.

Gary Snyder

Questions and Comments

1. A first consideration in reading any poem is our grasp of its
   plain sense. Note that Snyder's sense units often carry over to
   the lines below and end mid-line—a technique which slows
   the pace of the poem. But when you read the final five lines
   aloud you'll discover an easy flow of words, without pause.
   Is this change of pace suitable to the action described? Explain
   your answer.

2. List the evidence which the poet provides to fix the action in
   time and space. (Don't overlook the title!) How do lines 6–10,
   which mention the phases of the moon and Jupiter, contribute to the "fix"?

3. The theme of spring's urgent headway against winter's

stubborn hold is dramatized by images of warmth contrasted with images of cold. Comment on the appeal of these images to our various senses. They are central to the experience of the poem.

4. What does the mention of children and grandchildren in the final lines add to the poem?

from THE SONG OF SOLOMON

Rise up, my love, my fair one, and come away.
For, lo, the winter is past,
The rain is over and gone;
The flowers appear on the earth;
The time of the singing of birds is come,
And the voice of the turtle[1] is heard in our land;
The fig tree putteth forth her green figs,
And the vines with the tender grape give a good smell.
Arise, my love, my fair one, and come away.

Old Testament

Questions and Comments

1. What do you think is the mood of the speaker?

2. If you feel the touch of the breath of spring in these lines, the reason could be that the poet has created a contrast. What is the contrast?

3. The poet appeals to several of our senses. What are the sights, the smells, and the sounds of spring that he mentions?

4. With what do you associate doves? How do these associations enrich the poem?

[1] *turtle:* turtledove

THE PASTURE

I'm going out to clean the pasture spring;
I'll only stop to rake the leaves away
(And wait to watch the water clear, I may):
I sha'n't be gone long.—You come too.
I'm going out to fetch the little calf
That's standing by the mother. It's so young
It totters when she licks it with her tongue.
I sha'n't be gone long.—You come too.

Robert Frost

Questions and Comments

1. What sort of person do you guess the speaker to be? What does line 3 suggest about the speaker?

2. In what tone of voice might this poem be most effectively read aloud? Which words give the poem its conversational quality?

3. What invitation does the speaker give in this poem? Compare this poem with the selection from "The Song of Solomon" with respect to the nature of the invitation and the speaker's attitude toward the person addressed.

4. Robert Frost has begun several collections of his work with this poem. Does this placement of "The Pasture" suggest an additional kind of invitation? Explain your answer.

in Just-

in Just-
spring   when the world is mud-

luscious the little
lame balloonman

whistles   far   and   wee   5

and eddieandbill come
running from marbles and
piracies and it's
spring

when the world is puddle-wonderful   10

the queer
old balloonman whistles
far   and   wee
and bettyandisbel come dancing

from hop-scotch and jump-rope and   15

it's
spring
and
   the

      goat-footed   20

balloonMan   whistles
far
and
wee

                 e. e. cummings

Questions and Comments

1. When is "Just-spring"? According to the poem, what signals
   its arrival?

2. Which words and phrases suggest that in this poem the world
   is being viewed from the point of view of a child?

3. The typography of this poem—its arrangement on the page—is unusual. Assuming that the poet intends the poem's appearance to function as "stage directions" to the reader, how do you explain the strategy of running certain words together and of leaving extra spaces between other words?

4. Pan, the Greek god of woods, fields, flocks, and shepherds, was often represented as having the legs of a goat. He was also supposed to have loved music-making and dancing. What does the description of the "balloonman" as goat-footed and whistling add to the poem?

A LIGHT EXISTS IN SPRING

A light exists in spring
   Not present on the year
At any other period.
    When March is scarcely here

A color stands abroad   5
   On solitary hills
That science cannot overtake,
   But human nature *feels*.

It waits upon the lawn;
   It shows the furthest tree   10
Upon the furthest slope we know;
   It almost speaks to me.

Then, as horizons step,
   Or noons report away,
Without the formula of sound,   15
   It passes, and we stay:

A quality of loss

Affecting our content,
As trade had suddenly encroached
Upon a sacrament.   20

Emily Dickinson

Questions and Comments

1. Locate the main point of division in the poem. What action
takes place in the first section? In the second section?

2. What word in line 2 is unusual in this context? What word in
line 7? What words might be substituted to make the expression of these lines more ordinary? How do such words as
science and *formula* contrast with the rest of the language in
the poem?

3. What does the poet suggest by her use of the words *waits,
shows,* and *speaks* in the third stanza? In the next stanza do
you find "It passes, and we stay" a suitable conclusion? Why
or why not?

4. What is the loss in the situation which the speaker mentions
in the final two lines of the poem? Does the final word *sacrament* support the mood which the poet has established in the
earlier sections of the poem? Explain your answer.

dandelions

under cover of night and rain
the troops took over.
waking to total war in beleaguered houses
over breakfast we faced the batteries
marshalled by wall and stone, deployed   5
with a master strategy no one had suspected
and now all
firing

pow

all day, all yesterday   10
and all today
the barrage continued
deafening sight.
reeling now, eyes ringing from noise, from walking
gingerly over the mined lawns   15
exploded at every second
rocked back by the starshellfire
concussion of gold on green
bringing battle-fatigue
pow by lionface firefur pow by   20
goldburst shellshock pow by
whoosh   splat   splinteryellow   pow   by
pow   by   pow
tomorrow smoke drifts up
from the wrecked battalions,   25
all the ammunition, firegold fury, gone.
smoke
drifts
thistle-blown
over the war-zone, only   30

here and there, in the shade by the
peartree
pow   in the crack by the
curbstone   pow   and back of the
ashcan, lonely   35
guerrilla snipers, hoarding
their fire shrewdly
never

pow

surrender   40

Deborah Austin

11

Questions and Comments

1. What is the metaphor or comparison upon which this poem is based? Perhaps much of the charm of the poem lies in the many details with which the metaphor is developed. What are some of the details?

2. The visual sensations stirred by the scene have been expressed in images of sound. What instances do you find of the interplay of the two senses?

3. Which words seem to have been coined to assist in the creation of the poem's atmosphere? Explain the placement of the repeated "pows."

4. In what ways does the typography of the poem serve the poet's purpose as you see it?

HIGH TIDE

I edged back against the night.
The sea growled assault on the wave-bitten shore.
And the breakers,
Like young and impatient hounds,
Sprang with rough joy on the shrinking sand.
Sprang—but were drawn back slowly,
With a long, relentless pull,
Whimpering, into the dark.
Then I saw who held them captive;
And I saw how they were bound
With a broad and quivering leash of light,
Held by the moon,
As, calm and unsmiling,
She walked the deep fields of the sky.

Jean Starr Untermeyer

Questions and Comments

1. With what natural laws of our world does the poem deal?

2. The pictures in the poem have two aspects—what the speaker actually sees and what the speaker imagines. With which words is the basic *metaphor* introduced? Which words in the poem extend the comparison? Do you find the comparison effective in terms of the subject of the poem? Explain your answer.

3. Viewing the "I" in line 1 as you might a character in a play, what do you think is the feeling of the speaker in the first stanza? In the second stanza? If these feelings are different, how do you account for the change?

4. Does the poem succeed in evoking feelings in you? Explain your answer.

I TASTE A LIQUOR NEVER BREWED

I taste a liquor never brewed,
From tankards[1] scooped in pearl;
Not all the vats upon the Rhine
Yield such an alcohol!

Inebriate of air am I,   5
And debauchee of dew,
Reeling, through endless summer days,
From inns of molten blue.

When landlords turn the drunken bee
Out of the foxglove's door,   10
When butterflies renounce their drams,[2]
I shall but drink the more!

[1]*tankard:* a large drinking cup with a handle and, often, a hinged lid
[2]*dram:* (in this case) a small drink of liquor

Till seraphs swing their snowy hats,
And saints to windows run,
To see the little tippler 15
Leaning against the sun!

Emily Dickinson

Questions and Comments

1. The poem describes an unusual spree, to say the least. What actually is the "alcohol" drunk by the speaker?

2. What words and phrases develop the picture of drunkenness?

3. In what respects does the picture seem appropriate for the expression of the feeling with which this poem is charged?

4. How long will the spree continue? Give evidence from the poem.

5. What is implied by the interest in the "little tippler" displayed by the angels and saints? Is this what we could expect as the result of a drunken spree? Explain your answer.

HEAT

O wind, rend open the heat,
cut apart the heat,
rend it to tatters.

Fruit cannot drop
through this thick air— 5
fruit cannot fall into heat
that presses up and blunts
the points of pears
and rounds the grapes.

14

Cut through the heat—
plow through it,
turning it on either side
of your path.

H. D. (Hilda Doolittle)

Questions and Comments

1. With what physical characteristic has the poet endowed heat? How does this characteristic influence the action which is suggested in each of the three parts of the poem?

2. The basic action of cutting is common to the suggested comparisons in the first and last parts. How do the comparisons differ?

3. In the selection from "The Song of Solomon" we discovered that the smells and sounds of spring were the more appealing because the frozen sleep of winter was suggested (as a memory, perhaps). In this poem, what contrast seems to make the heat more oppressive?

APPARENTLY WITH NO SURPRISE

Apparently with no surprise
To any happy flower,
The frost beheads it at its play
In accidental power.

The blond assassin passes on,
The sun proceeds unmoved
To measure off another day
For an approving God.

Emily Dickinson

Questions and Comments

1. List the human qualities of the flower in this poem. What attitude does it have toward its own death?

2. Do sun and frost operate in league or against each other? According to the poem, what feeling does God have toward violence in His world?

3. Compare this poem with "Kyoto: March" as two poems which deal with the rhythm of the seasons.

Composition

1. What are the "rhythms in nature" which are presented in the poems in this section? Write a composition describing some aspect of the changing natural world not presented in the poems.

2. Write an essay in which you compare your "winter self" with your "summer self."

3. Emily Dickinson's "Apparently with No Surprise" calls attention to the rigorous war for survival going on within nature. Deborah Austin's "dandelions" suggests humanity's battle against one "natural enemy." Describe a struggle you have had against some natural element.

4. Reread Gary Snyder's "Kyoto: March." Try your hand at a similar poem by getting up fifteen minutes early tomorrow morning and going outdoors. See what the early light discovers, listen, open your pores to the air; then write down what you saw, heard, and felt.

THE ANIMAL WORLD

As we have looked about us in the world, frequently we have been fascinated by domesticated and wild animals. Why? Their needs and urges are often like ours. Certain mysteries hold us rapt: What do they think? What do they feel? And, of course, knowing that some of the wilder ones are killers heightens our awe as we try to guess at their inner lives.

The first four poems in this section deal with animals with which we are friendly; the remaining poems depict creatures toward which a few of us would move with uneasy caution and from which most of us would retreat with all deliberate haste.

HOUND ON THE CHURCH PORCH

The farmer knew each time a friend went past
Though he was deep in Sunday and his eyes
Were on the preacher or the azure squares
The high church sashes cut out of the skies
And on the dark blue serge upon his thighs.   5

Every time a man the farmer knew
Went by upon the road, the farmer's hound
On the church's wooden porch outside
Would thump his tail and make a pleasant sound,
His tail struck every time that it went round.   10

The farmer knew how well he knew each friend
Going by, he counted up the score;
If the passer-by were a plain friend,
There would be three thumps, or maybe four,
But if it was a good friend, there'd be more.   15

That would be Sam Rogers passing now,
And that must be Dave Merryman, all right,
For the hound-dog's joy flowed down his tail
And made it pound the planks with all its might,
He could not stop it going for delight.   20

The man in church sat back and glowed all through,
He heard the sermon, but it did not hide
The rhythm of the comforting old hymn
Of friendship that was going on outside,
And every inch of him belled out with pride.   25

Robert P. Tristram Coffin

Questions and Comments

1. Have you found yourself studying physical objects about you
   during an hour in church? What are some of the objects the
   farmer contemplates?

2. What details in stanzas 2, 3, and 4 develop the statement in
   the first line of the poem? How is the last stanza related to
   the first stanza?

3. Which lines in the poem appeal to your sense of hearing?

4. What emotion does the farmer feel?

5. The dog's actions may be interpreted as showing the same love of neighbor that the farmer feels while listening to the sermon inside the church. Do you agree with this interpretation? Why or why not? What words and phrases in the final stanza suggest the harmony between the activities going on inside the church and outside it?

THE RUNAWAY

Once when the snow of the year was beginning to fall,
We stopped by a mountain pasture to say, "Whose colt?"
A little Morgan[1] had one forefoot on the wall,
The other curled at his breast. He dipped his head
And snorted at us. And then he had to bolt.   5
We heard the miniature thunder where he fled,
And we saw him, or thought we saw him, dim and gray,
Like a shadow against the curtain of falling flakes.
"I think the little fellow's afraid of the snow.
He isn't winter-broken. It isn't play   10
With the little fellow at all. He's running away.
I doubt if even his mother could tell him, 'Sakes,
It's only weather.' He'd think she didn't know!
Where is his mother? He can't be out alone."
And now he comes again with clatter of stone,   15
And mounts the wall again with whited eyes
And all his tail that isn't hair up straight.
He shudders his coat as if to throw off flies.
"Whoever it is that leaves him out so late,
When other creatures have gone to stall and bin,   20
Ought to be told to come and take him in."

Robert Frost

---

[1] *Morgan:* a breed of light horses that originated in Vermont

19

Questions and Comments

1. Which phrases in the poem contribute to our awareness of where it takes place?

2. Which lines contain the most striking appeals to our senses? Which lines appeal to which senses?

3. From what do you think the colt is running away?

4. How do you account for the past tense in lines 1-8 and the change to the present tense in lines 15-18?

5. Note the direct quotations marked by single quotation marks (line 2, lines 9-14, lines 19-21) and double quotation marks (lines 12-13). Who is speaking in each case? What is the quoted speaker's feeling toward the colt? Is there a second feeling suggested in the unquoted sections of the poem? If you believe so, describe that feeling.

THE BRONCHO
THAT WOULD NOT BE BROKEN

A little colt—broncho, loaned to the farm
To be broken in time without fury or harm,
Yet black crows flew past you, shouting alarm,
Calling "Beware," with lugubrious¹ singing . . .
The butterflies there in the bush were romancing,   5
The smell of the grass caught your soul in a trance,
So why be a-fearing the spurs and the traces,
O broncho that would not be broken of dancing?

You were born with the pride of the lords great and olden
Who danced, through the ages, in corridors golden.   10
In all the wide farm-place the person most human.
You spoke out so plainly with squealing and capering,
With whinnying, snorting contorting and prancing,

¹*lugubrious:* mournful, very sad

20

As you dodged your pursuers, looking askance,
With Greek-footed figures, and Parthenon paces,[1]   15
O broncho that would not be broken of dancing.

The grasshoppers cheered. "Keep whirling," they said.
The insolent sparrows called from the shed
"If men will not laugh, make them wish they were dead."
But arch[2] were your thoughts, all malice displacing,   20
Though the horse-killers came, with snake-whips advancing.
You bantered and cantered away your last chance.
And they scourged you, with Hell in their speech and their
    faces,
O broncho that would not be broken of dancing.

"Nobody cares for you," rattled the crows,   25
As you dragged the whole reaper, next day, down the rows.
The three mules held back, yet you danced on your toes.
You pulled like a racer, and kept the mules chasing.
You tangled the harness with bright eyes side-glancing,
While the drunk driver bled you—a pole for a lance—   30
And the giant mules bit at you—keeping their places.
O broncho that would not be broken of dancing.

In that last afternoon your boyish heart broke.
The hot wind came down like a sledge-hammer stroke.
The blood-sucking flies to a rare feast awoke.   35
And they searched out your wounds, your death-warrant
    tracing.
And the merciful men, their religion enhancing,
Stopped the red reaper, to give you a chance.
Then you died on the prairie, and scorned all disgraces,
O broncho that would not be broken of dancing.   40

SOUVENIR OF GREAT BEND, KANSAS.   *Vachel Lindsay*

[1]*Parthenon paces:* in the manner of the horses carved on the Parthenon,
the temple of Athena at Athens.
[2]*arch:* clever; sly

Questions and Comments

1. The same line ends every stanza of the poem, marking the end of each scene in the drama of the young colt. How does each scene advance the total drama?

2. What hints of the tragic outcome are given earlier in the poem?

3. What parts in the drama do other living creatures (not human) play? What force do you think the mules represent?

4. Why do you think the colt is referred to as "the person most human" (line 11)? What attitude does the young horse seem to take toward his trainers (line 20)?

5. The use of words to express a meaning different from that which they ordinarily have is called "irony." What is ironic about line 37, "And the merciful men, their religion enhancing"?

6. Might this poem be interpreted as representing the conflict between the desire for freedom and the restraining power of civilization? Give reasons for your answer.

7. Compare the main idea of this poem with that of "The Runaway."

THE COW IN APPLE TIME

Something inspires the only cow of late
To make no more of a wall than an open gate,
And think no more of wall-builders than fools.
Her face is flecked with pomace and she drools
A cider syrup. Having tasted fruit,   5
She scorns a pasture withering to the root.
She runs from tree to tree where lie and sweeten
The windfalls spiked with stubble and worm-eaten.
She leaves them bitten when she has to fly.

She bellows on a knoll against the sky.   10
Her udder shrivels and the milk goes dry.

Robert Frost

Questions and Comments

1. If one should miss the cause for the cow's high spirits in the title, what other clues are found in the poem?

2. How does this picture of a drunkard compare with that given in Emily Dickinson's "I Taste a Liquor Never Brewed"?

3. Notice that the last three lines are separate sentences, the final words of which rhyme exactly. Do you think these concluding lines are effective in terms of what you see as the poet's purpose? Explain your answer.

THE BAT

By day the bat is cousin to the mouse.
He likes the attic of an aging house.

His fingers make a hat about his head.
His pulse beat is so slow we think him dead.

He loops in crazy figures half the night   5
Among the trees that face the corner light.

But when he brushes up against a screen,
We are afraid of what our eyes have seen:

For something is amiss or out of place
When mice with wings can wear a human face.   10

Theodore Roethke

Questions and Comments

1. How is the bat pictured in the first two stanzas? In the third and fourth stanzas?

2. What contributes to the conclusion that "something is amiss"? What is the climax to the growth of a sense of strangeness? How does the poet's word choice in the early stages of the poem foreshadow this climax?

3. Is this poem about a particular bat or about any bat? How do you account for your answer?

A NARROW FELLOW IN THE GRASS

A narrow fellow in the grass
Occasionally rides;
You may have met him,—did you not?
His notice sudden is.

The grass divides as with a comb,   5
A spotted shaft is seen;
And then it closes at your feet
And opens further on.

He likes a boggy acre,
A floor too cool for corn.   10
Yet when a child, and barefoot,
I more than once, at morn,

Have passed, I thought, a whip-lash
Unbraiding in the sun,—
When, stooping to secure it,   15
It wrinkled, and was gone.

Several of nature's people

I know, and they know me;
I feel for them a transport[1]
Of cordiality;   20

But never met this fellow,
Attended or alone,
Without a tighter breathing,
And zero at the bone.

Emily Dickinson

Questions and Comments

1. What "notice" does the narrow fellow in the grass give?

2. Where is the creature usually found? What exception does the word *yet* in line 11 introduce?

3. At what point in the poem did you realize that the narrow fellow was a snake?

4. What is the speaker's attitude toward snakes? How is this attitude revealed? What reason, if any, is given for this attitude? Compare the attitude toward one of nature's creatures in this poem and in "The Bat."

5. Point out examples of unexpected word usage and unusual images. What effects are given by such words and images?

THE EAGLE

He clasps the crag with crooked hands;
Close to the sun in lonely lands,
Ringed with the azure world, he stands.

The wrinkled sea beneath him crawls;

[1] *transport:* intense feeling

He watches from his mountain walls,
And like a thunderbolt he falls.

Alfred, Lord Tennyson

Questions and Comments

1. What living habits of the eagle do the images of the poem highlight? What qualities which we associate with the eagle do the images of the poem suggest?

2. According to one interpretation, the poem follows a basic rhythm in the life of a creature of prey—that of gathering power becoming striking power. How does the difference in the way the eagle is pictured in the first five lines and in the last line bear out this interpretation?

3. The first five lines may also be considered as setting a stage of vast space for the action of the last line. What words promote this effect? Might *azure* and *wrinkled* be among these words? If you think so, explain your answer.

4. The poet attributes some human characteristics to the eagle. Which words promote this effect? Might *walls* be one of these words? Might *crawls?* If you think so, explain your answer.

THE TIGER

Tiger, tiger, burning bright
In the forests of the night,
What immortal hand or eye
Could frame thy fearful symmetry?

In what distant deeps or skies   5
Burnt the fire of thine eyes?
On what wings dare he aspire?
What the hand dare seize the fire?

And what shoulder, and what art,
Could twist the sinews of thy heart?   10
And when thy heart began to beat,
What dread hand? and what dread feet?

What the hammer? what the chain?
In what furnace was thy brain?
What the anvil? What dread grasp   15
Dare its deadly terrors clasp?

When the stars threw down their spears,
And watered heaven with their tears,
Did He smile His work to see?
Did He who made the lamb, make thee?   20

Tiger, tiger, burning bright
In the forests of the night,
What immortal hand or eye
Dare frame thy fearful symmetry?

William Blake

Questions and Comments

This poem has puzzled and fascinated readers for more than one hundred years. Probably this is so because, although one may imagine a real beast in response to the poem, the images invite further associations of fearful power that can be felt far beyond the time and space of one jungle. The reference to the lamb in line 20 does spark associations of gentleness, goodness, or even holiness; and, prompted by the sense of the line, some readers have seen the tiger as a symbol of evil. Others argue that the force which the beast represents is awe-inspiring but not bad. Perhaps you will arrive at a different interpretation on the basis of evidence in the poem. "The Tiger" stands as an illustration of the notion that a great work of art has elements of inexhaustible mystery.

1. The main section of the poem is speculation concerning the identity of the tiger's maker. The creator is represented as being in what line of work? Which stanza furnishes the most evidence of this? Is the source of imagery appropriate in terms of what you see as the poet's purpose? Explain your answer.

2. You may interpret *symmetry* to mean "beauty." How does "fearful symmetry" apply to fire, one of the basic images of the poem, as well as to the tiger?

3. The word *dread* as it is repeated in lines 12 and 15 refers to the creator as well as to his creation. What do you think this reference suggests?

4. Do you find any change in intensity of feeling as you read from the first stanza to the fourth and then from the fourth to the fifth? If so, does the intensity of the feeling increase or decrease?

5. The last stanza is almost a repetition of the first. What is the effect of this repetition?

THE PANTHER

JARDIN DES PLANTES, PARIS

His sight from ever gazing through the bars
has grown so blunt that it sees nothing more.
It seems to him that thousands of bars are
before him, and behind them nothing merely.

The easy motion of his supple stride,   5
which turns about the very smallest circle,
is like a dance of strength about a center
in which a mighty will stands stupefied.

Only sometimes when the pupil's film
soundlessly opens . . . then one image fills   10

and glides through the quiet tension of the limbs
into the heart and ceases and is still.

Rainer Maria Rilke

Questions and Comments

It has been said that William Blake perhaps never saw a
tiger. Rilke's poem raises no such doubts about the experience
of the author. Not only does he mention a particular zoo in his
title, but also his descriptive details seem to grow out of careful
observation. In fact, his poem highlights one part of a cat's
anatomy of which you may not have been aware—the nictitat-
ing membrane ("the pupil's film" in line 9). This membrane
is a transparent eyelid beneath the outer lid, and it closes from
the inner corner of the eye across the pupil. In frogs and
chickens these protective membranes resemble transparent
windshield wipers. These eyelids in members of the cat family
are open more frequently than they are closed, but the poet
makes the opening seem to occur only occasionally.

1. What attribute of the panther is represented in the first
   stanza? What has blunted its sight? Why does it seem that
   there are "thousands of bars"?

2. What activity of the panther is the subject of the second stanza?
   Why is the "will stupified"?

3. In the third stanza the images of the first and second stanzas
   are combined. What do you think is the image the panther
   sees when the pupil's film is open and his vision is clear? Then
   what happens? Why?

4. The panther is presented from the point of view of a human
   observer. In what way do you think the statements about the
   captive panther might apply to humanity?

LOBSTERS IN THE WINDOW

First, you think they are dead.
Then you are almost sure
One is beginning to stir.
Out of the crushed ice, slow
As the hands on a schoolroom clock,   5
He lifts his one great claw
And holds it over his head;
Now he is trying to walk.

But like a run-down toy;
Like the backward crabs we boys   10
Waded for in the creek,
Trapped in jars or a net,
And then took home to keep.
Overgrown, retarded, weak,
He is fumbling yet   15
From the deep chill of his sleep

As if, in a glacial thaw,
Some ancient thing might wake
Sore and cold and stiff,
Struggling to raise one claw   20
Like a defiant fist;
Yet wavering, as if
Starting to swell and ache
With that thick peg in the wrist.

I should wave back, I guess.   25
But still in his permanent clench,
He's fallen back with the mass
Heaped in their common trench
Who stir, but do not look out

Through the rainstreaming glass,   30
Hear what the newsboys shout,
Or see the raincoats pass.

W. D. Snodgrass

Questions and Comments

1. Compare the point of view from which the action is described with that of "The Panther." What do we learn about the speaker of this poem?

2. Which words describing the lobster might apply to human beings? Which metaphors (or comparisons) do you find most helpful in visualizing the lobsters? What associations do you have in response to the image of "some ancient thing" waking?

3. Like the panther of the preceding poem, the lobsters face a barrier to freedom beyond which is a strange human world. Discuss the poet's treatment of the two worlds.

Composition

1. With reference to "The Cow in Apple Time," recount the most humorous situation you can recall in which an animal was the main character.

2. "The Runaway" and "The Broncho That Would Not Be Broken" have something to say about "civilized" treatment of young horses. Write a composition in which you demonstrate people's thoughtlessness in dealing with natural creatures.

3. Vachel Lindsay's "The Broncho That Would Not Be Broken" also makes some symbolic suggestion about the education of human beings. Henry Adams in *The Education of Henry Adams* had this to say on the subject: "A boy's will is his life, and he dies when it is broken, as the colt dies in harness, taking a new nature in becoming tame. Rarely has the boy felt kindly

towards his tamers. Between him and his master has always been war. Henry Adams never knew a boy of his generation to like a master, and the task of remaining on friendly terms with one's own family, in such a relation, was never easy." Discuss this statement in terms of your own experience.

4. "Hound on the Church Porch" depicts a man's having a religious experience which was not designed by the preacher. Have you had an educational experience which was not designed by a teacher? If so, describe it.

THE CITY AND BEYOND

As human beings, through technology, have gained more and more control of their environment, grass and trees have been slowly disappearing. Great cities rise; machines drone over and around us; yet poets remain and, seizing upon images of our industrial culture, continue to find beauty and to make their comments on the human situation.

Under the smoke and in the shadows of tall buildings, other older images, however, persist. The call of the open road, the pull of the ocean tides are felt. Some poets respond by becoming vagabonds; others travel the hills of their imagination.

Most of the poems in this section focus upon life in the cities; the rest represent the incitement of wanderlust or the contemplation of cool retreat.

COMPOSED UPON
WESTMINSTER BRIDGE

Earth has not anything to show more fair:
Dull would he be of soul who could pass by
A sight so touching in its majesty:

This City now doth like a garment wear
The beauty of the morning; silent, bare,   5
Ships, towers, domes, theaters and temples lie
Open unto the fields, and to the sky;
All bright and glittering in the smokeless air.
Never did sun more beautifully steep
In his first splendor, valley, rock, or hill;   10
Ne'er saw I, never felt, a calm so deep!
The river glideth at his own sweet will:
Dear God! the very houses seem asleep;
And all that mighty heart is lying still!

William Wordsworth

Questions and Comments

1. Which lines show what the speaker actually sees? Which lines show the speaker's feelings when looking upon the scene?

2. One might state that Wordsworth compares the city to a person. What evidence in the poem can you find to support that statement?

3. Show how the poem might be considered to move from pictures of surface serenity to suggestions of inner peace.

A PIPER

A piper in the street to-day,
Set up, and tuned, and started to play,
And away, away, away on the tide
Of his music we started; on every side
Doors and windows were opened wide,   5
And men left down their work and came,

And women with petticoats coloured like flame,
And little bare feet that were blue with cold,
Went dancing back to the age of gold,
And all the world went gay, went gay,   10
For half an hour in the street to-day.

Seumas O'Sullivan

Questions and Comments

1. The final line of the poem tells us the fun lasted for half an hour. What inferences do you make about ordinary life in the community?

2. A piper can symbolize musicians, poets, and artists, who though their media create fresh forms and speak to the human spirit. How might the action of this poem be a concrete instance of the role of the artist?

3. In keeping with the subject, the language is not conversational as is that of Wordsworth's sonnet. It swings; it has a beat. O'Sullivan manages this effect by his arrangement of syllables. Frequently strong stresses recur after two unaccented syllables—most evident in lines 7 and 8:

> Ănd wómĕn wĭth pĕttĭcŏats cóloŭred lĭke fláme,

> Ănd líttlĕ băre feét thăt wĕre blúe wĭth cóld.

Find other instances of this metrical variation among the more common *iambs* (units or feet containing two syllables the second of which receives major stress). Iambic feet, for instance, predominate in line 6.

SPARKLES FROM THE WHEEL

Where the city's ceaseless crowd moves on the livelong
    day,

35

Withdrawn I join a group of children watching, I
    pause aside with them.

By the curb toward the edge of the flagging,
A knife-grinder works at his wheel sharpening a great
    knife,
Bending over he carefully holds it to the stone, by
    foot and knee,   5
With measur'd tread he turns rapidly, as he presses
    with light but firm hand,
Forth issue then in copious golden jets,
Sparkles from the wheel.

The scene and all its belongings, how they seize and
    affect me,
The sad sharp-chinn'd old man with worn clothes and
    broad shoulder-band of leather,   10
Myself effusing and fluid, a phantom curiously
    floating, now here absorb'd and arrested,
The group, (an unminded point set in a vast
    surrounding,)
The attentive, quiet children, the loud, proud, restive
    base of the streets,
The low hoarse purr of the whirling stone, the light-
    press'd blade,
Diffusing, dropping, sideways-darting, in tiny
    showers of gold,   15
Sparkles from the wheel.

Walt Whitman

Questions and Comments

1. This poem's structure is common in the lyric tradition: a
   description of a scene followed by the speaker's reflection
   upon it. How is the second part of the poem an imaginative
   extension of the first part?

2. How important is the city's ongoing hum, the small audience in relation to the central image of the knife grinder at work? Explain your answer.

3. How might lives of individuals be like "sparkles from the wheel"? Note that Whitman describes himself as "a phantom curiously floating."

4. In the preceding poem a piper, like the "balloonman" in "in Just-", temporarily changes the community he enters. Explain how the knife grinder performs a similar function.

ON BROADWAY

About me young and careless feet
Linger along the garish street;
   Above, a hundred shouting signs
Shed down their bright fantastic glow
   Upon the merry crowd and lines   5
Of moving carriages below.
Oh wonderful is Broadway—only
My heart, my heart is lonely.

Desire naked, linked with Passion,
Goes strutting by in brazen fashion;   10
   From playhouse, cabaret and inn
The rainbow lights of Broadway blaze
   All gay without, all glad within.
As in a dream I stand and gaze
At Broadway, shining Broadway—only   15
My heart, my heart is lonely.

Claude McKay

Questions and Comments

1. From what vantage point is the speaker surveying the scene? What time of day is it? Are the images appropriate to the place and time? Explain your answer. How is the speaker's situation different from that in Wordsworth's poem "Composed Upon Westminster Bridge"? What influence does the situation seem to have on the selection of imagery in each poem?

2. What attitude toward the city do you think is shown in the first stanza until the dash in line 7? What attitude is shown in the second stanza until the dash in line 15?

3. What contrast does the last line of each stanza offer? How do you account for this contrast?

IN A STATION OF THE METRO

The apparition of these faces in the crowd;
Petals on a wet, black bough.

Ezra Pound

Questions and Comments

Would you call two lines that do not rhyme a poem? If the images they create register in our minds and suggest a pattern of feeling to us, two lines can be a poem!

Pound described his inspiration for the poem as his delight at seeing one lovely face after another in a Paris subway station. His first effort to record his feelings was thirty lines long. A year later, he settled for this haiku[1]-like statement.

[1]*Haiku:* a Japanese verse form consisting of three lines totaling 17 syllables

1. The title of the poem—the subway system of Paris is called "the Metro"—helps to explain the metaphor posed by the two lines. What are the corresponding elements in the comparison which the poem implies? What do the "petals" correspond to? What does the "black bough" correspond to?

2. What does the poet gain by using the word *apparition* rather than *appearance?*

3. What feeling toward the subway crowd do you think is suggested by the poem? Do you find that the feeling for the city surroundings in this poem is different from that in "On Broadway"? Explain your answer.

THE HARBOR

Passing through huddled and ugly walls
By doorways where women
Looked from their hunger-deep eyes,
Haunted with shadows of hunger-hands,
Out from the huddled and ugly walls,   5
I came sudden, at the city's edge,
On a blue burst of lake,
Long lake waves breaking under the sun
On a spray-flung curve of shore;
And a fluttering storm of gulls,   10
Masses of great gray wings
And flying white bellies
Veering and wheeling free in the open.

Carl Sandburg

Questions and Comments

1. What are the "walls" through which the speaker passes? What does the word *walls* suggest to you? What feeling is suggested

by the first five lines of the poem? Do you notice a narrowing of the field of vision in these lines? What is in the center of the picture?

2. What happens to the speaker's field of vision in the remaining lines of the poem? What feeling is suggested in these lines?

3. What contrasts in light and shadow can you find in the poem? What contrasts in line and shape? In motion?

4. Harbors form a line dividing civilization from the unexplored sea. Comment on divisions listed in the poem.

going uptown to visit miriam

on the train
old ladies playing football
going for empty seats

very funny persons

the train riders   5
                  are silly people
                  I am a train rider

but no one knows where I am
going to take this train

to take this train   10
to take this train

the ladies   read popular
paperbacks   because they
are popular   they get off

40

at 42 to change for the   15
westside line   or off
59 for the department store

the train pulls in & out
the white walls   darkness   white walls   dark-   20
ness

ladies look up   i
wonder where they are going
the dentist   pick up
husband pick up wife   25
pick up kids
pick up ?grass?
to library   to museum
to laundromat   to school

but no one knows where i am   30
going to take this train

to take this train

to visit miriam
to visit miriam

& to kiss her   35
on the cheek
& hope i don't
see sonia on the
street

But no one knows where i'm taking 40
this train
        taking this train
        to visit miriam.

Victor Hernandez Cruz

Questions and Comments

1. In your own words describe the speaker's state of mind.

2. Our trains of thought frequently switch tracks involuntarily and then return to a happy clickety-clack. With what techniques does Cruz suggest the flow of consciousness? In what ways might the rhythms and shape of the poem suggest the passage of the subway train itself?

3. What attitudes toward life in the city does the poem convey? Compare the speaker's feelings for the people on the train with those of the speaker in "In a Station of the Metro."

MERRITT PARKWAY

As if it were
forever that they move, that we
keep moving—

    Under a wan sky where
    as the lights went on a star   5
      pierced the haze & now
    follows steadily
        a constant
    above our six lanes
    the dreamlike continuum... 10

And the people—ourselves!
 the humans from inside the
 cars, apparent
 only at gasoline stops
       unsure,   15
  eyeing each other

     drink coffee hastily at the

                    slot machines & hurry
           back to the cars
                    vanish   20
                    into them forever, to
                    keep moving—

Houses now & then beyond the
sealed road, the trees / trees, bushes   25
passing by, passing
           the cars that
                    keep moving ahead of
           us, past us, pressing behind us
                                        and
                    over left, those that come   30
           toward us shining too brightly
moving relentlessly

           in six lanes, gliding
           north & south, speeding with
           a slurred sound—   35

                    Denise Levertov

Questions and Comments

1. Highway travel, the poem implies, brings out an aura of
unreality, a dissolving of identity. Do you find this true from
your own experience? If so, account for these effects.

2. It is said that the characters in our dreams are projections
of ourselves. Where is there a mixing of third person and
first person in the poem? How else does the poet communicate "the dreamlike continuum"? Which words are repeated?
Comment on the final phrase—"speeding with/a slurred
sound—."

3. How are the people characterized at the "gasoline stops"?
Contrast this attitude toward one's traveling companions with

43

that implied in "going uptown to visit miriam." Comment on the fact that the subway riders are going *somewhere*, whereas the Merritt Parkway riders seem to have no origin or destination.

TRAVEL

The railroad track is miles away,
    And the day is loud with voices speaking,
Yet there isn't a train goes by all day
    But I hear its whistle shrieking.

All night there isn't a train goes by,   5
    Though the night is still for sleep and dreaming,
But I see its cinders red on the sky,
    And hear its engine steaming.

My heart is warm with the friends I make,
    And better friends I'll not be knowing;   10
Yet there isn't a train I wouldn't take,
    No matter where it's going.

Edna St. Vincent Millay

Questions and Comments

1. What is the time of day in the first stanza? What contrasts with the sound of the train?

2. What is the time of day in the second stanza? What contrasts with the sound of the train? What visual image is included in this stanza? Is it appropriate? Why or why not?

3. What contrasts with the train in the third stanza?

4. Analyze the rhyme scheme of the poem. Notice that the rhymes at the ends of the second and fourth lines in each stanza involve a stressed next-to-the-last syllable and an unstressed final syllable.

44

The desire for a change of scene can have any of several causes. What do you think is behind the urge to get away in this poem? How does the motivation differ from that in "The Harbor"?

I LIKE TO SEE IT LAP THE MILES

I like to see it lap the miles,
And lick the valleys up,
And stop to feed itself at tanks;
And then, prodigious, step

Around a pile of mountains,   5
And, supercilious, peer
In shanties by the sides of roads;
And then a quarry pare

To fit its sides, and crawl between,
Complaining all the while   10
In horrid, hooting stanza;
Then chase itself down hill

And neigh like Boanerges;[1]
Then, punctual as a star,
Stop—docile and omnipotent—   15
At its own stable door.

Emily Dickinson

Questions and Comments

1. What is the metaphor that is the basis of the poem? What

[1] *Boanerges:* from the Hebrew, meaning "sons of thunder"; any bellowing preacher or orator

actions of the machine-animal in each stanza develop the metaphor? Do you find the image of the animal chasing itself down hill to be appropriate? Explain.

2. What adjective in the first stanza is applied to the machine-animal? Notice the other big adjectives in lines 6 and 15. What is similar about the use of these adjectives? What concrete images accompany each of the adjectives? What is contradictory about the pairing of *docile* and *omnipotent?*

3. In each of the first three stanzas the final line is nonstop; in other words, the sense unit it begins is not concluded with the final line but continues, sending the reader on to the next stanza without a pause. In what way is this pattern suited to the topic being treated?

THE LAKE ISLE OF INNISFREE

I will arise and go now, and go to Innisfree,
And a small cabin build there, of clay and wattles made:
Nine bean-rows will I have there, a hive for the honey-bee,
And live alone in the bee-loud glade.

And I shall have some peace there, for peace comes dropping
    slow,   5
Dropping from the veils of the morning to where the cricket
    sings;
There midnight's all a glimmer, and noon a purple glow,
And evening full of the linnet's wings.

I will arise and go now, for always night and day
I hear lake water lapping with low sounds by the shore;   10
While I stand on the roadway, or on the pavements grey,
I hear it in the deep heart's core.

William Butler Yeats

Questions and Comments

1. What activities are contemplated in the first stanza of the poem? What aspect of life at Innisfree is presented in the second stanza? What situation is suggested in the final two lines?

2. What is the dominant mood of the poem? How does the contrast in the final two lines relate to the mood which has been established?

3. What images in the poem appeal to the visual sense? To the sense of hearing? What kind of image predominates? How does this predominance relate to the mood of the poem?

4. Explain the basic metaphor contained in lines 5 and 6.

HEAVEN-HAVEN

A nun takes the veil

I have desired to go
　　Where springs not fail,
To fields where flies no sharp and sided hail,
　　And a few lilies blow.

And I have asked to be
　　Where no storms come,
Where the green swell is in the havens dumb,
　　And out of the swing of the sea.

Gerard Manley Hopkins

Questions and Comments

1. From what does the speaker seek haven in the first stanza? In the second stanza? Why do you think the place the speaker wishes to go is described only in terms of what isn't there?

2. What does the subtitle add to your understanding of the poem? How does it extend the references to springs, sharp and sided hail, storms, green swell, swing of the sea, and lilies?

3. In what ways are the language patterns of the two stanzas similar?

Composition

1. Write a composition in which you consider the idea that old cities are better than new ones. You may agree or disagree.

2. Write a composition in which you consider the idea that suburbia combines the best features of city living and of country living. You may agree or disagree.

3. Seek out a high physical vantage point in your town or city and climb there during the early morning or evening; then write a poem or essay which expresses the appearance and character of the city as you see it.

4. Emily Dickinson wrote at a time when the steam locomotive was most stupendous means for the conquest of space. The locomotive's appeal to her imagination is demonstrated in "I Like to See It Lap the Miles." Write a poem or essay in which you present an imaginative picture of one of our twentieth-century vehicles.

5. Select two poems from this section which clearly vary in their attitude toward civilization, and write a composition in which you analyze and contrast these attitudes.

YOUTH AND AGE

The poems in this section deal with growth and changes in us. Some of the poems deal with the complex feelings of children as they try to relate to members of the adult world, and some of the poems deal with the equally complex feelings of adults trying to relate to children. The last three poems reckon with the passage of time from birth to death.

FIRST LESSON

Lie back, daughter, let your head
be tipped back in the cup of my hand.
Gently, and I will hold you. Spread
your arms wide, lie out on the stream
and look high at the gulls. A dead-   5
man's float is face down. You will dive
and swim soon enough where this tidewater
ebbs to the sea. Daughter, believe
me, when you tire on the long thrash
to your island, lie up, and survive.   10
As you float now, where I held you

and let you go, remember when fear
cramps your heart, what I told you:
lie gently and wide to the light-year
stars, lie back, and the sea will hold you.   15

Philip Booth

Questions and Comments

1. In which line do you note a change in voice quality that
   would suggest the parent's unspoken thought as opposed
   to direct address? Contrast the use of "the gulls" in line 5
   with that of "the light-year stars" (lines 14 and 15).

2. At what point in the poem do we realize the lesson deals
   with more than swimming? How old do you guess the daughter is? At what age might she profit from the second phase
   of the lesson?

3. State in your own words the substance of lines 9–15. How do
   you interpret "your island" in line 10?

4. As stressed earlier, one of the poet's chief means of involving
   the reader is imagery—representation of sense experience.
   List the words and phrases which incite in you the sense of
   relaxation and flotation.

THE SECRET HEART

Across the years he could recall
His father one way best of all.

In the stillest hour of night
The boy awakened to a light.

Half in dreams, he saw his sire   5
With his great hands full of fire.

The man had struck a match to see
If his son slept peacefully.

He held his palms each side the spark
His love had kindled in the dark.   10

His two hands were curved apart
In the semblance of a heart.

He wore, it seemed to his small son,
A bare heart on his hidden one,

A heart that gave out such a glow   15
No son awake could bear to know.

It showed a look upon a face
Too tender for the day to trace.

One instant, it lit all about,
And then the secret heart went out.   20

But it shone long enough for one
To know that hands held up the sun.

Robert P. Tristram Coffin

Questions and Comments

1. What incident is the poem relating? Are we informed of the reason for the father's visit to his son's bedroom? If so, in what line? Give your account for the tenderness of his look. In what sense had love lit the match as is stated in line 10?

2. With reference to line 16, why might a son awake not be able to bear such a look on his father's face? Does anything in the poem suggest that the father might disguise his feelings during the daytime? Explain. Do you find this picture of a father-son relationship to be a realistic one? Explain.

3. Occasionally we have "moments of enlightenment" which have a lasting significance. Yet the meaning of such moments is seldom easy to express. Here the poet uses language which does not make sense, when taken literally, to suggest the impact on the boy of seeing his father's secret heart. How do you interpret the boy's impression that "hands held up the sun"?

MY PAPA'S WALTZ

The whiskey on your breath
Could make a small boy dizzy;
But I hung on like death:
Such waltzing was not easy.

We romped until the pans   5
Slid from the kitchen shelf;
My mother's countenance
Could not unfrown itself.

The hand that held my wrist
Was battered on one knuckle;   10
At every step you missed
My right ear scraped a buckle.

You beat time on my head
With a palm caked hard by dirt,
Then waltzed me off to bed   15
Still clinging to your shirt.

Theodore Roethke

Questions and Comments

1. Which words in the poem call up images of motion? Of muscular tension?

2. Characterize the father as fully as you can from evidence within the poem. Could the waltz, for such a man, be an expression of love? Explain.

3. Where does the speaker stand in time in relation to the incident presented in the poem? In "The Secret Heart" the passage of time lent significance to a childhood incident. Can you make a similar case for "My Papa's Waltz"? In your answer tell what you think the boy's attitude was at the time of the incident and how his attitude may have changed with the passing of the years.

CHILD ON TOP OF A GREENHOUSE

The wind billowing out the seat of my britches,
My feet crackling splinters of glass and dried putty,
The half-grown chrysanthemums staring up like accusers,
Up through the streaked glass, flashing with sunlight,
A few white clouds all rushing eastward,
A line of elms plunging and tossing like horses,
And everyone, everyone pointing up and shouting!

Theodore Roethke

Questions and Comments

1. How would you guess the child came to be on the greenhouse roof? Why do you suppose the chrysanthemums stare like accusers? In what respects does the child's world seem different from this new vantage point?

2. The focus of the child's vision shifts several times. In what lines do these shifts occur?

3. Do you find any appeals to other senses besides the visual

sense? If so, in which lines? What words and phrases suggest
the force of the wind?

ELEVEN

And summer mornings the mute child, rebellious,
Stupid, hating the words, the meanings, hating
The Think now, Think, the O but Think! would leave
On tiptoe the three chairs on the verandah
And crossing tree by tree the empty lawn   5
Push back the shed door and upon the sill
Stand pressing out the sunlight from his eyes
And enter and with outstretched fingers feel
The grindstone and behind it the bare wall
And turn and in the corner on the cool   10
Hard earth sit listening. And one by one,
Out of the dazzled shadow in the room
The shapes would gather, the brown plowshare, spades,
Mattocks, the polished helves of picks, a scythe
Hung from the rafters, shovels, slender tines   15
Glinting across the curve of sickles—shapes
Older than men were, the wise tools, the iron
Friendly with earth. And sit there quiet, breathing
The harsh dry smell of withered bulbs, the faint
Odor of dung, the silence. And outside   20
Beyond the half-shut door the blind leaves
And the corn moving. And at noon would come,
Up from the garden, his hard crooked hands
Gentle with earth, his knees still earth-stained, smelling
Of sun, of summer, the old gardener, like   25
A priest, like an interpreter, and bend
Over his baskets.
                    And they would not speak:
They would say nothing. And the child would sit there
Happy as though he had no name, as though   30

54

He had been no one: like a leaf, a stem,
Like a root growing—

Archibald MacLeish

Questions and Comments

1. To what does the title refer?

2. Explain the situation. What is the boy rebelling against? What action does he take?

3. What brings happiness to the boy? In what way is the old gardener a priest or an interpreter to the boy? How can not having a name and being like a growing leaf, stem, or root be seen as a happy state?

4. Explain how shapes might "gather" (line 13). How do you interpret the phrase "shapes older than men were" (lines 16-17)? What associations might the words "iron friendly with earth" bring to mind?

5. To which of the senses are appeals made? Which lines in the poem make the different appeals?

YOUTH'S PROGRESS

Dick Schneider of Wisconsin . . . was elected "Greek God" for an interfraternity ball.—Life.

When I was born, my mother taped my ears
So they lay flat. When I had aged ten years,
My teeth were firmly braced and much improved.
Two years went by; my tonsils were removed.

At fourteen, I began to comb my hair   5
A fancy way. Though nothing much was there,
I shaved my upper lip—next year, my chin.
At seventeen, the freckles left my skin.

Just turned nineteen, a nicely molded lad,
I said goodbye to Sis and Mother; Dad   10
Drove me to Wisconsin and set me loose.
At twenty-one, I was elected Zeus.[1]

John Updike

Questions and Comments

1. What seems to be the poet's basis for selecting milestones
along the path of the youth's journey? Does the seeming
seriousness of the title "Youth's Progress" contribute to the
comic effect of the poem? If so, why? The quotation from
the now defunct *Life* magazine evidently "inspired" the
poem. How is it helpful to the reader?

2. At what do you think the poet is poking fun in this poem?

old age sticks

old age sticks
up Keep
Off
signs)&

youth yanks them   5
down(old
age
cries No

Tres)&(pas)
youth laughs   10
(sing
old age

[1] *Zeus:* chief god of the ancient Greeks, ruler of the heavens and of all
human beings

scolds Forbid
den Stop
Must   15
n't Don't

&)youth goes
right on
gr
owing old   20

    e. e. cummings

Questions and Comments

1. Does this poem express a universal truth? Explain the tendency of older people to restrict the energies of the young. Do you detect any irony, or unexpected outcome, in the final statement? Explain your answer.

2. Are you still "yanking signs down"? Have you put any up lately—on your bedroom door? Are there any other signs of your growing old?

3. What do Cummings' lining and typography add to the expression of feeling? Comment on any suggested second meanings of *sticks, owing old.* Are the parentheses consistent and appropriate? The capitalization?

THE DAY

The day was a year at first
When children ran in the garden;
The day shrank down to a month
When the boys played ball.

The day was a week thereafter   5
When young men walked in the garden;
The day was itself a day
When love grew tall.

The day shrank down to an hour
When old men limped in the garden;   10
The day will last forever
When it is nothing at all.

Theodore Spencer

Questions and Comments

1. The phrase "in the garden" makes a regular appearance in the poem. What action takes place in the garden at each stage? What progression do you detect in the actions? How is the day described at each stage? Relate the progression of the actions to the acceleration in the passage of time which the poem presents.

2. What other examples of repetition can you find in the poem?

3. How do you explain the poet's equating "nothing" with "forever" in the last two lines?

4. Compare the treatment of growth and decline in "The Day" with that in "old age sticks." Comment on the voice of the speaker in each case.

SOLOMON GRUNDY

Solomon Grundy,
Born on Monday,
Christened on Tuesday,
Married on Wednesday,

Took ill on Thursday,   5
Worse on Friday,
Died on Saturday,
Buried on Sunday;
This is the end
Of Solomon Grundy.   10

Mother Goose

Questions and Comments

1. If you were to divide one's lifetime into seven equivalent segments, which of life's experiences would you allot to each segment?

2. What attitude toward life is suggested by this nursery rhyme? How does it differ from that suggested in Theodore Spencer's "The Day"?

3. Do you think the name "Solomon Grundy" is an appropriate one? Why or why not?

MEDITATION ON HIS NINETY-FIRST YEAR

This withered clutch of bones, this hand that held
Two oxen and a plow steadily down
An even furrow, now scarcely can hold
The heavy reading-glass. An April sun
Could bring me to a sweat when my thin blood   5
Was warmer; now I'm tissue dry and shake
In any breeze that giddies this grey head.
"The years have flown," a fellow patriarch
Is fond of saying, but as I reflect
Upon nine decades ripening steadily,   10
Each measured year maturing, act by act,

I wonder at him—could his memory
Remain so barren that life disappears
Into a limbo of forgotten years?

It's pleasant for me now to spin the past: 15
A boyhood full of cows and berry vines,
Hay-ricks and wild birds, the journey west
When I was seventeen, the evergreens
And rivers and the rocks . . . I took a wife
The fall that my first crop was harvested,   20
And in our cabin, under a pitch-caulked roof,
We bred four sons out of our strongest blood.
I've planted every year, yet never known
Two springs so much alike I could not tell
One from the other; no two days have been   25
Identical, and I can still recall
Each acre tilled, each crop or foal or calf . . .
The living things—these are my epitaph.

The doctor tells me I should not expect
To live forever. After he has gone   30
I smile to think that he, at thirty-eight,
Cannot conceive how well, at ninety-one,
I have accepted this absurd remark.
Today the teacup chatters at my teeth;
I feel the room grow colder, and I break   35
With reveries and vague regrets that growth
Is over, that the blood wears out, and then
No more of things that breathe and climb, no more.
But, though I feel the minutes growing thin
And I've torn the last page from the calendar,   40
I cannot grudge the passing of my breath—
After so much of life, so little death.

John Haag

Questions and Comments

1. The following words may be unfamiliar to you: *giddies* (line 7), *patriarch* (line 8), *limbo* (line 14), *foal* (line 27), *absurd* (line 33). What does each mean in its context?

2. How does the poet represent the passage of time in the first seven lines?

3. A fellow patriarch says, "The years have flown" (line 8). In contrast, how does the speaker regard the passage of time?

4. What images of the past, held in the speaker's memory, show that he has not permitted his life to disappear "into a limbo of forgotten years"? What does he mean when he says "The living things—these are my epitaph" (line 28)?

5. What images in the first stanza are echoed by words or phrases in the last stanza? What lines tie in with "The living things—these are my epitaph" in the second stanza?

6. In "Born Yesterday," the first poem in this section, a wish is made for a child, a wish for a "skilled, vigilant, flexible, unemphasised, enthralled catching of happiness." Do you think the speaker's life in "Meditation on His Ninety-first Year" demonstrates a catching of happiness? Explain your answer.

Composition

1. With reference to "Youth's Progress" young and older Americans are often persistent seekers after good looks and popularity. Do these attributes promote the growth of happiness? Are there other qualities which make the achievement of happiness more certain? Write a composition in which you explain your view of these matters.

2. With reference to "Meditation on his Ninety-first Year," compare the opportunities for mental satisfaction in jobs in which a worker can see a product take form (such as farming or carpentry) with opportunities for mental satisfaction in other types of work.

3. Have you ever had a moment of clear communication with a person a number of years younger or a number of years older than you—a situation in which the difference in age didn't seem to matter? If so, write a description of this situation.

4. If you had an opportunity to "skip" adolescence in the process of growing up, would you accept the "promotion"? Explain your answer in composition form.

5. A singular fact of life is change—change in ourselves, as well as change in our friends. What kind of person do you think, or hope, you will be when you reach the age of your parents?

6. The following quotation has been attributed to Oscar Wilde: "When we're young, we obey our parents; later we judge them; later still, we forgive them, sometimes." From the experience of your own life, discuss the validity of this statement.

IN AND OUT OF LOVE

What is love and what is romance? What is love and what is selfishness?

Just as the scientist probes the mysteries of the physical world, the poet explores the mysteries of the human heart. In the poems of this section we will see love as joyous anticipation, as heartbreaking disappointment, and finally as everlasting affection.

NEXT DOOR

My neighbors on the right
Have a young son who has just
Commenced to step out.
My neighbors on the left
Have a young daughter   5
Who is still a virgin.
In the heavy shadow
Under the gate it is very dark
After the sun has set.
Whose head is that, looking over the wall?   10

Mei Yao Ch'en

Questions and Comments

1. Recreate the situation of the poem from the point of view of the girl or the boy. Compare the feeling expressed in your version with that of the original.

2. Roughly how old is the speaker of "Next Door"? Describe the speaker's attitude toward the neighbors, toward young love. Could it be that the speaker is engaging in a little peeping?

3. Analyze the structure, commenting on the arrangement of sentences—the substance and length of each.

4. The first three sentences, you've discovered, share a grammatical similarity. Against this syntactic rhythm, what effect is generated by the last line?

THE DATE

She woke up
glad at last
out of dreams
           bouncing
from the cool   5
sheets in April,
and leaning
far O far
out the window
with the blue curtains   10
                flying
in pigtails
in the travelling wind
around
the white house   15
and the tumbling barn
and straw-buried hens,

saw
the new light
roll   20
along the green meadows
and in the early clover,
saw
the new light
roll   25
like a golden gasoline,

saw
the birds
ignite in time
from juicy points of trees.   30

Leaning
far O far
out the window
                    she heard
Him tooting,   35
and the world turn over
like a smooth machine.

David Lyttle

Questions and Comments

1. How old do you think the subject of the poem is? If we view this poem as a portrayal of the waking from the sleep of childhood into the growing awareness of adolescence, what significance do you see in the words "at last" in line 2 and "the new light" in line 19?

2. What period of her life is suggested by the images in lines 12–17? Explain why these images take on an unreal or dream-like quality. Note that in line 3 the poet says that she woke "out of dreams."

3. What emotions are expressed in such images as "green meadows," "early clover," "juicy points of trees," and finally the
   image of the world turning over? How do you interpret "the
   birds ignite in time" (lines 26-27)? Are there additional in-
   terpretations which are valid? Do you find the images which
   refer to automobiles appropriate? Why or why not?

4. Note the colors that appear in the poem. How might the order
   in which these colors appear be related to the central idea of
   the poem?

MEETING AT NIGHT

The gray sea and the long black land;
And the yellow half-moon large and low;
And the startled little waves that leap
In fiery ringlets from their sleep,
As I gain the cove with pushing prow,   5
And quench its speed i' the slushy sand.

Then a mile of warm sea-scented beach;
Three fields to cross till a farm appears;
A tap at the pane, the quick sharp scratch
And blue spurt of a lighted match,   10
And a voice less loud through its joys and fears,
Than the two hearts beating each to each!

Robert Browning

Questions and Comments

1. This poem and "The Date" focus upon the period of time
   shortly before a meeting. At what point in each work did you
   become aware that the action of the poem centers upon the
   reunion of members of the opposite sex? In what way do the

dramatic situations of the two poems differ? Discuss the difference in the speaker's physical point of view in the two poems.

2. Notice that the first stanza of "Meeting at Night" deals with the journey on water and the second, with the journey on land. What images suggest the sea in the first stanza? What images suggest the land in the second stanza?

3. We see brightness breaking against a backdrop of darkness in each stanza. Which lines contain the images of fire? What do the rhymes of these lines contribute to the poem? How might this pattern of imagery be appropriate to the subject of the poem?

RONDEAU

Jenny kissed me when we met,
   Jumping from the chair she sat in;
Time, you thief, who love to get
   Sweets into your list, put that in!
Say I'm weary, say I'm sad,
   Say that health and wealth have missed me,
Say I'm growing old; but add—
   Jenny kissed me!

Leigh Hunt

Questions and Comments

A *rondeau* is a French verse form which takes its refrain from the beginning of the first line.

1. This poem spotlights a single kiss. Do you regard the kiss as representing a long love affair? Why or why not? What do you gather is the relationship between the speaker and Jenny? At what time in the speaker's life do you believe the kiss took place? Explain your answer.

2. What impression do you have of the speaker from his words and from the feelings he reveals?

3. Notice the lively turns supplied by the rhymes at the end of lines 2, 4, 6, and 8. What other elements in the poem contribute to its lightness and its joyous movement?

THE KISS

I hoped that he would love me,
    And he has kissed my mouth,
But I am like a stricken bird
    That cannot reach the south.

For though I know he loves me,
    To-night my heart is sad;
His kiss was not so wonderful
    As all the dreams I had.

Sara Teasdale

Questions and Comments

1. In the previous poem, "Rondeau," we saw the reaction of one person to a kiss. The speaker in this poem suggests that a kiss can lead to an entirely different effect. What feeling does each speaker have concerning the kiss?

2. Can we say that one or the other of the speakers in the two poems has touched a psychological truth? Can we say that, given a particular set of circumstances, each speaker is correct? What might the circumstances be?

THE LICORICE FIELDS AT PONTEFRACT

In the licorice fields at Pontefract
  My love and I did meet
And many a burdened licorice bush
  Was blooming round our feet;
Red hair she had and golden skin,   5
Her sulky lips were shaped for sin,
Her sturdy legs were flannel-slack'd,
The strongest legs in Pontefract.

The light and dangling licorice flowers
  Gave off the sweetest smells;   10
From various black Victorian towers
  The Sunday evening bells
Came pealing over dales and hills
And tanneries and silten mills
And lowly streets where country stops   15
And little shuttered corner shops.

She cast her blazing eyes on me
  And plucked a licorice leaf;
I was her captive slave and she
  My red-haired robber chief.   20
Oh love! for love I could not speak,
It left me winded, wilting, weak
And held in brown arms strong and bare
And wound with flaming ropes of hair.

John Betjeman

Questions and Comments

1. How did the red-haired woman and the licorice blossoms seem to work together in affecting the speaker?

2. To which earlier statement does the "ropes of hair" image in the last line relate?

3. How might line 21 ("O love! for love I could not speak") be read aloud to give the best interpretation of the word *love*?

4. Lines 11 through 16 create a mood which contrasts with the rest of the poem. Discuss this contrast and its value.

5. This poem could remind us of traditional English love ballads that deal with springtime frolics and/or the powers of beautiful women—even of the traditional diction of such poetry. Does anything in the characterization or setting seem to go against romantic convention? Explain your answer.

THE PICNIC

It is the picnic with Ruth in the spring.
Ruth was third on my list of seven girls
But the first two were gone (Betty) or else
Had someone (Ellen has accepted Doug).
Indian Gully the last day of school;   5
Girls make the lunches for the boys too.
I wrote a note to Ruth in algebra class
Day before the test. She smiled, and nodded.
We left the cars and walked through the young corn
The shoots green as paint and the leaves like tongues 10
Trembling. Beyond the fence where we stood
Some wild strawberry flowered by an elm tree
And Jack-in-the-pulpit was olive ripe.
A blackbird fled as I crossed, and showed
A spot of gold or red under its quick wing.   15
I held the wire for Ruth and watched the whip
Of her long, striped skirt as she followed.
Three freckles blossomed on her thin, white back
Underneath the loop where the blouse buttoned.
We went for our lunch away from the rest,   20
Stretched in the new grass, our heads close

Over unknown things wrapped up in wax papers.
Ruth tried for the same, I forget what it was,
And our hands were together. She laughed,
And a breeze caught the edge of her little   25
Collar and the edge of her brown, loose hair
That touched my cheek. I turned my face in-
to the gentle fall. I saw how sweet it smelled.
She didn't move her head or take her hand.
I felt a soft caving in my stomach   30
As at the top of the highest slide
When I had been a child, but was not afraid,
And did not know why my eyes moved with wet
As I brushed her cheek with my lips and brushed
Her lips with my own lips. She said to me   35
Jack, Jack, different than I had ever heard,
Because she wasn't calling me, I think,
Or telling me. She used my name to
Talk in another way I wanted to know.
She laughed again and then she took her hand;   40
I gave her what we both had touched—can't
Remember what it was, and we ate the lunch.
Afterward we walked in the small, cool creek
Our shoes off, her skirt hitched, and she smiling,
My pants rolled, and then we climbed up the high   45
Side of Indian Gully and looked
Where we had been, our hands together again.
It was then some bright thing came in my eyes,
Starting at the back of them and flowing
Suddenly through my head and down my arms   50
And stomach and my bare legs that seemed not
To stop in feet, not to feel the red earth
Of the Gully, as though we hung in a
Touch of birds. There was a word in my throat
With the feeling and I knew the first time   55
What it meant and I said, it's beautiful.
Yes, she said, and I felt the sound and word
In my hand join the sound and word in hers

As in one name said, or in one cupped hand.
We put back on our shoes and socks and we   60
Sat in the grass awhile, crosslegged, under
A blowing tree, not saying anything.
And Ruth played with shells she found in the creek,
As I watched. Her small wrist which was so sweet
To me turned by her breast and the shells dropped   65
Green, white, blue, easily into her lap,
Passing light through themselves. She gave the pale
Shells to me, and got up and touched her hips
With her light hands, and we walked down slowly
To play the school games with the others.   70

John Logan

Questions and Comments

1. How old are the main characters? What seems to be the speaker's attitude toward the outing before it takes place? How does this attitude change by the poem's end? Comment on the choice of words in the concluding line: "To play the school games with the others."

2. Which descriptive passages did you find most striking? To which specific senses do they appeal?

3. Some of our most important feelings cannot be put into words. Logan's characters seem to acknowledge the inadequacy of language; nonetheless, through intonation, touch, and other non-verbal means, they communicate. At what points did they communicate without words?

RECUERDO

We were very tired, we were very merry—
We had gone back and forth all night on the ferry.

It was bare and bright, and smelled like a stable—
But we looked into a fire, we leaned across a table,
We lay on a hill-top underneath the moon; 5
And the whistles kept blowing, and the dawn came soon.

We were very tired, we were very merry—
We had gone back and forth all night on the ferry;
And you ate an apple, and I ate a pear,
From a dozen of each we had bought somewhere; 10
And the sky went wan, and the wind came cold,
And the sun rose dripping, a bucketful of gold.

We were very tired, we were very merry,
We had gone back and forth all night on the ferry.
We hailed, "Good morrow, mother!" to a shawl-covered
head, 15
And bought a morning paper, which neither of us read;
And she wept, "God bless you!" for the apples and pears,
And we gave her all our money but our subway fares.

Edna St. Vincent Millay

Questions and Comments

1. We get to know the two people in the poem primarily from their activities of one night. What can we infer about this couple from the evidence given in the poem?

2. *Recuerdo* is Spanish for *remembrance*. What are some of the factors which you believe make the night memorable for the speaker?

3. What is the mood of the poem? What words in particular help to create this mood? How do the repeated lines contribute to the mood?

4. To which of our senses do the images of the poem appeal? Which images appeal to which senses?

5. What incident is recounted in the last stanza of the poem?

Why does an act of generosity and kindness seem to be a fitting ending to this night?

IF I SHOULD LEARN

If I should learn, in some quite casual way,
That you were gone, not to return again—
Read from the back-page of a paper, say,
Held by a neighbor in a subway train,
How at the corner of this avenue   5
And such a street (so are the papers filled)
A hurrying man, who happened to be you,
At noon today had happened to be killed—
I should not cry aloud—I could not cry
Aloud, or wring my hands in such a place—   10
I should but watch the station lights rush by
With a more careful interest on my face;
Or raise my eyes and read with greater care
Where to store furs and how to treat the hair.

Edna St. Vincent Millay

Questions and Comments

1. Do you think the speaker loves the person being addressed? Why or why not?

2. Line 9 and 10 suggest that she would yield to her grief in private. Why not on a subway train? With reference to the final four lines, what physical or psychological therapy can derive from careful, disciplined study of one's surroundings?

3. In the history of literature the sonnet has been a popular vehicle for the expression of love. But the meter and rhymes

of a sonnet's fourteen lines must conform to particular patterns, creating challenging limitations for the poet. Because Millay has managed the effect of natural conversation building to intense drama within this form, she ranks as one of the most accomplished sonneteers of the English language. Find other love sonnets of hers in your library.

STRANGE FITS OF PASSION
HAVE I KNOWN

Strange fits of passion have I known:
And I will dare to tell,
But in the Lover's ear alone,
What once to me befell.

When she I loved looked every day   5
Fresh as a rose in June,
I to her cottage bent my way,
Beneath an evening-moon.

Upon the moon I fixed my eye,
All over the wide lea;[1]   10
With quickening pace my horse drew nigh
Those paths so dear to me.

And now we reached the orchard-plot;
And, as we climbed the hill,
The sinking moon to Lucy's cot[2]   15
Came near, and nearer still.

In one of those sweet dreams I slept,
Kind Nature's gentlest boon!

[1] *lea:* a meadow   [2] *cot:* cottage

And all the while my eyes I kept
On the descending moon.   20

My horse moved on; hoof after hoof
He raised, and never stopped:
When down behind the cottage roof,
At once, the bright moon dropped.

What fond[1] and wayward thoughts will slide   25
Into a Lover's head!
"O mercy!" to myself I cried,
"If Lucy should be dead!"

William Wordsworth

Questions and Comments

1. Why does the speaker want to restrict his audience to lovers only (line 3)?

2. Fits of passion may be of various kinds. What form does this one take? In what sense may thoughts be "wayward" (line 25)?

3. What association do we have with the moon that makes it appropriate as a symbol in this poem? Why should the moon be a more appropriate symbol than a star would be in terms of the unexpected turn at the end of the poem?

4. How many times is the word *moon* used in the poem? What words describe the movement of the moon as the speaker slowly approaches Lucy's cottage? Is there any progression in these adjectives which modify *moon*? What arguments can you make for the moon and Lucy's having become one and the same in the speaker's mind?

5. This poem and the preceding one illustrate how the possibilities of a loved one's death can haunt a person. How do you explain this phenomenon?

___

[1] *fond:* foolish

SHE DWELT AMONG
THE UNTRODDEN WAYS

She dwelt among the untrodden ways
  Beside the springs of Dove,[1]
A Maid whom there were none to praise
  And very few to love:

A violet by a mossy stone   5
  Half hidden from the eye!
—Fair as a star, when only one
  Is shining in the sky.

She lived unknown, and few could know
  When Lucy ceased to be;   10
But she is in her grave, and, oh,
  The difference to me!

William Wordsworth

Questions and Comments

1. What grammatical relationship do the last two lines of the first stanza have with the first two lines? What is the grammatical relationship of the second stanza to the first?

2. What words and phrases suggest the seclusion of Lucy's life? What evidence is there in the poem that Lucy lived in harmony with nature?

3. Which stanza contains the most vivid appeals to our senses? To what sense are the appeals made? At the heart of the poem lie two striking comparisons. In the first one, to what is Lucy compared? In the second? Discuss the aptness of these metaphors in terms of what you know about Lucy.

4. How does the placement of *oh* in line 11 emphasize line 12?

[1] *Dove:* a stream in the Midlands of England

O MISTRESS MINE,
WHERE ARE YOU ROAMING?

O mistress mine, where are you roaming?
O stay and hear; your true love's coming,
   That can sing both high and low:
Trip no further, pretty sweeting;
   Journeys end in lovers' meeting,   5
   Every wise man's son doth know.

What is love? 'tis not hereafter;
Present mirth hath present laughter;
   What's to come is still[1] unsure:
In delay there lies no plenty;   10
Then come kiss me, sweet and twenty,[2]
   Youth's a stuff will not endure.

William Shakespeare

Questions and Comments

This song is taken from a drinking scene in the comedy *Twelfth Night* during which two tipsy old knights call for a love song from Feste, the clown or court fool.

1. To whom do you think the poem is addressed?

2. What idea is presented in the second stanza? What is the relationship of the second stanza to the first?

3. Besides being entertaining, Shakespeare's clowns reveal sensitivities to the harsh and sad sides of life. Do you find that the tone of merriment in this song is mixed with a tone of wistfulness? If so, what elements in the poem itself suggest this additional attitude?

---

[1] *still:* always   [2] *sweet and twenty:* with reference to the girl—ordinary sweetness multiplied by twenty

SONNET XXIX

When in disgrace with fortune and men's eyes,
I all alone beweep my outcast state,
And trouble deaf Heaven with my bootless[1] cries,
And look upon myself, and curse my fate,
Wishing me like to one more rich in hope,   5
Featur'd like him, like him with friends possess'd,
Desiring this man's art, and that man's scope,
With what I most enjoy contented least;
Yet in these thoughts myself almost despising,
Haply[2] I think on thee,—and then my state   10
Like to the lark at break of day arising
From sullen earth sings hymns at heaven's gate;
   For thy sweet love remember'd such wealth brings,
   That then I scorn to change my state with kings.

William Shakespeare

Questions and Comments

A *sonnet* is a popular verse form consisting of fourteen lines which have a set rhyme scheme. Frequently, an idea is introduced in the first eight lines and concluded in the final six lines. A sonnet which you have encountered earlier in the book is Wordsworth's "Composed Upon Westminster Bridge."

1. The semicolon at the end of line 8 marks the end of the first part of the poem. In your own words summarize the thought of the first eight lines. The final six lines establish a contrast. Express the thought of these lines in your own words.

2. Compare the feelings which are established in the two parts of the poem.

3. How many times is the word *state* used in the poem? What is the meaning of the word in each instance of its use?

4. Do you feel that the last two lines are necessary? At what other point might the poem have ended? Explain your answer.

---

[1] *bootless:* useless   [2] *Haply:* by luck or chance

WHEN YOU'RE AWAY

When you're away, I'm restless, lonely,
Wretched, bored, dejected; only
Here's the rub, my darling dear,
I feel the same when you are near.

Samuel Hoffenstein

Questions and Comments

1. What humorous effect is achieved in this poem? What technique does the poet use to achieve it?

2. At what way of looking at life does this poem seem to be poking fun?

SONG

Why so pale and wan, fond lover?
   Prithee, why so pale?
Will, when looking well can't move her,
   Looking ill prevail?
Prithee[1], why so pale?   5

Why so dull and mute, young sinner?
   Prithee, why so mute?
Will, when speaking well can't win her,
   Saying nothing do't?
Prithee, why so mute?   10

Quit, quit, for shame, this will not move:
   This cannot take her.
If of herself she will not love,
   Nothing can make her:
   The devil take her!   *John Suckling*

[1]*Prithee:* I pray thee (tell me)

Questions and Comments

The rhyme scheme of this poem is an elaborate one, especially considering that in the early seventeenth century, when it was written, *love* and *move* rhymed, each having the vowel sound that *move* has in present-day English.

1. What is the attitude of the speaker toward the young man addressed? Toward the young woman involved? Compare the speaker's attitude toward unrequited love to that of the speaker in "O Mistress Mine, Where Are You Roaming?".

2. Do you think the appeal of this poem is logical or emotional? Explain your choice.

3. This poem contains various kinds of repetition. What are some of these?

LORD RANDAL

"Oh where hae[1] ye been, Lord Randal, my son?
O where hae ye been, my handsome young man?"
"I hae been to the wild wood; mother, make my bed soon,
For I'm weary wi[2] hunting and fain wald[3] lie down."

"Where gat[4] ye your dinner, Lord Randal, my son?   5
"Where gat ye your dinner, my handsome young man?"
"I din'd wi my true-love; mother, make my bed soon,
For I'm weary wi hunting, and fail wald lie down."

"What gat ye to your dinner, Lord Randal, my son?
What gat ye to your dinner, my handsome young man?"   10
"I gat eels boiled in broo;[5] mother, make my bed soon,
For I'm weary wi hunting and fain wald lie down."

[1]*hae:* have   [2]*wi:* of; with   [3]*fain wald:* would rather   [4]*gat:* got
[5]*broo:* broth

"What became of your bloodhounds, Lord Randal, my
    son?
What became of your bloodhounds, my handsome
    young man?"
"O they swell'd and they died; mother, make my bed
    soon,   15
For I'm weary wi hunting, and fain wald lie down."

"Oh I fear ye are poison'd, Lord Randal, my son!
O I fear ye are poison'd, my handsome young man!"
"Oh yes! I am poison'd; mother, make my bed soon,
For I'm sick at the heart, and I fain wald lie down."   20

Traditional

Questions and Comments

    This ballad and the one which follows it, with their stories
of intrigue and violent deeds, are typical of English and
American folk tradition. The characters speak for themselves,
and the stories move to their climaxes with a minimum of
details. "Lord Randal" affords its readers dialogue only,
whereas both "Lord Randal" and "Flora, the Lily of the
West" have refrains as binders to each stanza.

1. Who are the two speakers in this ballad? From their conversa-
    tion, what do you learn has actually taken place? Why would
    you guess Lord Randal was poisoned? What do you guess
    about the relationships of mother, son, and sweetheart?

2. What effect does the refrain as it recurs have on the emotional
    tension of this ballad? What words does the mother repeat
    over and over again? What predominant mood emerges as a
    result of all this repetition? What is the effect of the substitu-
    tion of "I'm sick at the heart" for "I'm weary wi hunting" in
    the final stanza?

FLORA, THE LILY OF THE WEST

When first I came to Louisville
  My fortune there to find,
I met a fair young maiden there.
  Her beauty filled my mind;
Her rosy cheek, her ruby lips—   5
  They gave my heart no rest.
The name she bore was Flora,
  The Lily of the West.

I courted lovely Flora;
  She promised ne'er to go;   10
But soon a tale was told to me
  That filled my heart with woe.
They said she meets another man,
  Who holds my love in jest.
And yet I trusted Flora,   15
  The Lily of the West.

Way down in yonder shady grove—
  A man of low degree—
He spoke unto my Flora there
  And kissed her 'neath the tree.   20
The answers that she gave to him,
  Like arrows, pierced my breast.
I was betrayed by Flora,
  The Lily of the West.

I stepped up to my rival,   25
  My dagger in my hand;
I seized him by the collar
  And I ordered him to stand.
All in my desperation,
  J stabbed him in his breast.   30
I killed a man for Flora,
  The Lily of the West.

And then I had to stand my trial;
   I had to make my plea;
They placed me in a prisoner's dock   35
   And then commenced on me.
Although she swore my life away,
   Deprived me of my rest,
Still I loved my faithless Flora,
   The Lily of the West.   40

Traditional

Questions and Comments

1. What do you think are the speaker's present surroundings? How is his attitude toward unrequited love different from the attitudes revealed by the speaker in "Song"? Do you consider this speaker's attitude believable? Explain your answer.

2. What is the story that the speaker relates? Compare the amount of detail supplied to you in this ballad and that supplied in "Lord Randal." Which ballad is more satisfying to you? Why?

3. Note the refrain that appears in the last two lines of every stanza. What effect does this refrain have on the mood of the ballad? What comparison can you make between the mood of this ballad and that of "Lord Randal"?

WHEN YOU ARE OLD

When you are old and grey and full of sleep,
And nodding by the fire, take down this book,
And slowly read, and dream of the soft look
Your eyes had once, and of their shadows deep;

How many loved your moments of glad grace,   5
And loved your beauty with love false or true,
But one man loved the pilgrim soul in you,
And loved the sorrows of your changing face;

And bending down beside the glowing bars,
Murmur, a little sadly, how Love fled   10
And paced upon the mountains overhead
And hid his face amid a crowd of stars.

William Butler Yeats

Questions and Comments

Notice that the poem is one sentence. It is reasonable to interpret the second stanza as a continuation of the reverie which started in line 3. In the final stanza the woman's action by the fireside resumes, and *murmur* has the same subject (*you* understood) which the verbs *take, read,* and *dream* have in the first stanza.

1. What do you guess are the ages of the man and the woman at the time he is speaking? Explain your answer. What do you suppose has taken place between the man and the woman?

2. To what might "this book" (line 2) refer? To whom might "one man" (line 7) refer? What sort of soul might a "pilgrim soul" (line 7) be? If we take "glowing bars" (line 9) to refer to the grate containing the fire, at what stage, most likely, is the fire? How does this image support the thought of the poem?

3. Do you regard this poem as a bitter explosion designed to hurt the person to whom it is addressed? Why or why not? In what kind of speaking voice might the poem be most effectively read?

4. How do you explain the last two lines of the poem?

A DEEP-SWORN VOW

Others because you did not keep
That deep-sworn vow have been friends of mine;
Yet always when I look death in the face,
When I clamber to the heights of sleep,
Or when I grow excited with wine,
Suddenly I meet your face.

William Butler Yeats

Questions and Comments

1. The speaker refers to an ill-fated love affair of the past. How long a period of time would you say has elapsed since the love affair ended? What evidence within the poem supports your belief? Whom does the speaker blame for the break-up? What evidence within the poem supports your view?

2. What change do you detect between lines 2 and 3 in the speaker's attitude toward the former lover?

3. What is significant about the circumstances under which the speaker sees the face of a former lover? What sort of experiences might be referred to by "when I look death in the face"? It does seem that the speaker has been trying to forget a former lover. How do you account for the lover's being recalled upon the occasion mentioned?

4. What is your opinion of the effectiveness of the last line ?

WHEN TROUT SWIM DOWN
GREAT ORMOND STREET

When trout swim down Great Ormond Street,[1]
And sea-gulls cry above them lightly,

[1] *Great Ormond Street:* a street in a fashionable section of London

And hawthorns heave cold flagstones up
To blossom whitely,

Against old walls of houses there,   5
Gustily shaking out in moonlight
Their country sweetness on sweet air;
And in the sunlight,

By the green margin of that water,
Children dip white feet and shout,   10
Casting nets in the braided water
To catch the trout:

Then I shall hold my breath and die,
Swearing I never loved you; no,
"You were not lovely!" I shall cry,   15
"I never loved you so."

Conrad Aiken

Questions and Comments

1. Notice the word *then* introducing the last stanza. How does
the last stanza complete the statement begun with the first line
of the poem?

2. What turn of events does line 1 suggest? What turn of events
does line 3 suggest? How do the scenic elements in the re-
mainder of the first three stanzas contrast with those of lines
2 and 3?

3. At what point did you realize that this is a love poem? What
is unusual about the way the speaker makes a declaration of
love? How might the idea of this poem be stated in somewhat
more prosaic form?

4. What similarities in feeling do you note between this poem
and "A Deep-Sworn Vow"?

Composition

1. Going steady, according to many parents, is undesirable for adolescents. Write an essay which clearly explains your view of the matter.

2. With reference to "Rondeau" by Leigh Hunt and "The Kiss" by Sara Teasdale, what events in your life have been happier to look back on than they were to look ahead to? What events in your life were more attractive to look ahead to than they have been to look back on? Discuss these events and account for the differences in your feelings about them.

3. Which of the poems in this section seems to you to be the happiest "in love" poem? Which seems to be the saddest "out of love" poem? Write two short compositions defending your choices.

4. With reference to either "Lord Randal" or "Flora, the Lily of the West," write a news story concerning the situation which the poem represents. Base your story on the facts to which a reporter would probably have access.

PORTRAITS

Riding in the subway or in buses, how often have you wished to know the stories behind the faces of certain people? Unlike fiction, which creates complete histories of characters, poetry grants its readers glimpses and hints to ponder—somewhat more in keeping with your subway observations.

You should enjoy this collection of fourteen portraits, each of which reveals to some degree a secret life beyond the appearance.

EVERY GOOD BOY DOES FINE

I practiced my cornet in a cold garage
Where I could blast it till the oil in drums
Boomed back; tossed free-throws till I couldn't move my
    thumbs;
Sprinted through tires, tackling a headless dummy.

In my first contest, playing a wobbly solo,   5
I blew up in the coda, alone on stage,

And twisting like my hand-tied necktie, saw the judge
Letting my silence dwindle down his scale.

At my first basketball game, gangling away from home
A hundred miles by bus to a dressing room, 10
Under the showering voice of the coach, I stood in a towel,
Having forgotten shoes, socks, uniform.

In my first football game, the first play under the lights
I intercepted a pass. For seventy yards I ran
Through music and squeals, surging, lifting my cleats, 15
Only to be brought down by the safety man.

I took my second chances with less care, but in dreams
I saw the bald judge slumped in the front row,
The coach and team at the doorway, the safety man
Galloping loud at my heels. They watch me now. 20

You who have always horned your way through passages,
Sat safe on the bench while some came naked to court,
Slipped out of arms to win in the long run,
Consider this poem a failure, sprawling flat on a page.

David Wagoner

Questions and Comments

1. In what way does the first stanza prepare you for stanzas 2, 3,
   and 4? Give line references. What parallels in sentence con-
   struction do you find in stanzas 2, 3, and 4? Point out examples of parallel constructions elsewhere in the poem.

2. How is the word *gangling* used in line 9? What similarly unusual use of words do you find elsewhere in the poem?

3. How would you describe the boy's attitude toward practice
   for his various performances? Is there any relationship between this attitude and his reaction to the cited instances?
   Explain.

4. How do you interpret line 17? What did the speaker learn from his first "chances"? How is the fifth stanza related to stanzas 2, 3, and 4? How do you interpret "They watch me now" (line 20)?

5. How is the last stanza related to the preceding stanzas? What second meanings are suggested to you by the poet's use of the words *horned, passages, bench, court,* and *long run* in this stanza? Why might this poem, or possibly any poem, be considered a failure by the sort of person depicted in the final stanza?

6. Probably, from your own experience with music, you recognize E(very) G(ood) B(oy) D(oes) F(ine) in the title to be the lines of the musical staff *going up* the scale. Considering the images of falling which recur in the poem, do you find this to be an appropriate title? Why or why not?

I'M NOBODY! WHO ARE YOU?

I'm nobody! Who are you?
Are you nobody, too?
Then there's a pair of us—don't tell!
They'd banish us, you know.

How dreary to be somebody!
How public, like a frog
To tell your name the livelong day
To an admiring bog!

Emily Dickinson

Questions and Comments

1. Why should being nobody be kept secret? To whom do you think *they* refers in the fourth line?

2. What do you think is the speaker's attitude toward fame? Compare this attitude with that suggested in the last stanza of David Wagoner's "Every Good Boy Does Fine."

3. What are some circumstances under which it is desirable to be "nobody"? Relate your answer to the circumstances depicted in Archibald Macleish's "Eleven."

LAKE OF BAYS

"Well, I'm not chicken..."
that skinny ten-year old girl
balanced on the crazy-high railing
of the Dorset bridge:
                              suddenly   5
let go down
fifty feet into the water.

"That one will never grow up
to be a lady," my mother said
as we walked away;   10

but I'll remember
her brown body dropping like a stone
long after I've forgotten
many many ladies...

Raymond Souster

Questions and Comments

1. Why is the girl's action memorable for the speaker, who doesn't know her personally and probably never will? What does she symbolize?

2. Do you find the poem itself memorable? If so, why?

3. Characterize the "voice qualities" of the girl's "Well, I'm not chicken . . ." in contrast to the mother's reaction. How do the two quotations highlight a universal conflict between classes? Between generations?

GERT SWASEY

Have you ever asked yourselves—ladies, ladies—what it
    must have been like
To have been Gert Swasey?
To have a rich father,
To run away from home
To be a circus queen, and   5
To come back a charlady?
To come home and be old?
Dirty and old?

Few of you now can remember Gert Swasey
When she was young—how she was young: 10
What was it like do you suppose
To drive through town as though you thumbed your
    nose,
Your red hair flying, and beautiful clothes?
What was it like to want to do that
Seventy years ago—ladies, ladies?   15
Gert was a wild one, and when she wanted
She'd drive a pair of horses like a witch enchanted.
She'd drive them down from Mount Washington
As though she were fired out of a cannon;
And all the way along Merrimac,   20
Up Main, through Summer Street, down Mill and back
Till she charted up the driveway of her father's
    mansion,
Twice around where the iron stag stared,

Then as fast to the coach-house as she dared
Which was twice as fast as anybody dared;   25
The horses snorting and all in lather,
But there was nothing Gert would rather
Than set the whole downtown awhirl
Gasping at that Swasey girl.

I wonder how it was to be that Swasey girl   30
Not a Sanders nor a Dow nor a Saltonstall,
But a new-rich Irish with no family at all
Save a sporting father who kept a stable.
It must have been both mad and sweet
To thunder through leaf-filled Summer Street   35
Disturbing the ladies at the tea table,
Disturbing the ladies in the summer house,
And all along Merrimac's shops and factories
The men's quick faces.

Then to run away—to run far away   40
To ride in a circus—
The colored wheels
The tights and spangles
The lights, the crowd
The wonderful horses,   45
The plumed, proud, wonderful white horses,
The tremendous music.
To travel like a gypsy
To dress like a queen
To see all the world that she'd never seen   50
That was never the world where she had been.
Not a Dow nor a Sanders nor a Saltonstall
Unless they paid to get in
And then
After thirty-five years to come home again.   55

Have you ever asked yourselves what it must have been
        like

94

To be the old charlady at the B. & M. railroad station?
To clean the toilets
To mop the floors
To be greasy and gray   60
To be poor and alone
To be Gert Swasey?
Then there is a way easy to learn—
Of talking to yourself,
Answering yourself,   65
When there is no one else
Wherever you are.
There are many stray cats, a dozen—fifty—
That will stay in your house
If you will feed them,   70
Lock them in to keep then safe,
Whose yowling some day wakes the neighborhood
But, at last, not you.
Have you ever asked yourselves what it must have been
    like
To have been Gert Swasey?   75
To be a rich young nobody with red restless hair?
To run away from home
To be a circus queen, and
To come back,
And to be old, and to be dirty, and to be dead—   80
O, ladies, ladies.

Winfield Townley Scott

Questions and Comments

1. From the evidence in the poem what sort of person was Gert
Swasey? Why do you think she behaved as she did?

2. The speaker has strong feelings about the "ladies" being
addressed. How are the socially proper folk of the present
linked to an earlier generation? Why might the speaker want
them to empathize with Gert?

3. Cite some of the images or other poetic techniques which affect you and make Gert Swasey a memorable character.

TO HELEN

Helen, thy beauty is to me
   Like those Nicean[1] barks of yore,
That gently, o'er a perfumed sea,
   The weary, way-worn wanderer bore
   To his own native shore.   5

On desperate seas long wont to roam,
   Thy hyacinth hair, thy classic face,
Thy Naiad[2] airs have brought me home
   To the glory that was Greece
And the grandeur that was Rome.   10

Lo! in yon brilliant window-niche
   How statue-like I see thee stand!
   The agate lamp within thy hand,
Ah! Psyche,[3] from the regions which
   Are Holy Land!   15

Edgar Allan Poe

Questions and Comments

Poe believed that movement, sound, color, and feeling should combine in a poem to create a particular mood. "To Helen" seems to stand as an embodiment of his theory because in the poem we have more clearly the creation of a mood than we do the portrait of a human being. It might have been, for

[1] *Nicean:* of an ancient people who sailed the Mediterranean
[2] *Naiad:* a water nymph
[3] *Psyche:* a maiden whose beauty was envied by Venus. She was made immortal by Jupiter and personifies the soul.

instance, that Poe used the word *hyacinth* (line 7) as much for the sound of the word and its Greek origin as he did for either of the lexical meanings it could have for us—that of gems or flowers. Finally, when he calls his subject "Psyche" (line 14), he elevates her to an immortal purity and beauty toward which all the images of the poem seem to move.

The first two stanzas of the poem establish a fairly elaborate metaphor. With what is Helen compared? With what is the speaker compared?

EX-BASKETBALL PLAYER

Pearl Avenue runs past the high school lot,
Bends with the trolley tracks, and stops, cut off
Before it has a chance to go two blocks,
At Colonel McComsky Plaza. Berth's Garage
Is on the corner facing west, and there,   5
Most days, you'll find Flick Webb, who helps Berth out.

Flick stands tall among the idiot pumps—
Five on a side, the old bubble-head style,
Their rubber elbows hanging loose and low.
One's nostrils are two S's, and his eyes   10
An E and O. And one is squat, without
A head at all—more of a football type.

Once, Flick played for the high school team, the
    Wizards.
He was good: in fact, the best. In '46,
He bucketed three hundred ninety points,   15
A county record still. The ball loved Flick.
I saw him rack up thirty-eight or forty
In one home game. His hands were like wild birds.

He never learned a trade; he just sells gas,
Checks oil, and changes flats. Once in a while,   20
As a gag, he dribbles an inner tube,
But most of us remember anyway.
His hands are fine and nervous on the lug wrench.
It makes no difference to the lug wrench, though.

Off work, he hangs around Mae's Luncheonette.   25
Grease-grey and kind of coiled, he plays pinball,
Sips lemon cokes, and smokes those thin cigars;
Flick seldom speaks to Mae, just sits and nods
Beyond her face towards bright applauding tiers
Of Necco Wafers, Nibs, and Juju Beads.   30

John Updike

Questions and Comments

1. The poem is energized by the contrast between past and present. What kind of basketball player was Flick? What kind of garage attendant is he? How does the poet refer to Flick's hands—then and now?

2. Of the five stanzas, which is devoted to Flick's glorious past? How might line 7 ("Flick stands tall among the idiot pumps") give further meaning to the poem's structure?

3. Explain the metaphor created by "applauding tiers" in the next-to-last line?

4. Describe the speaker's attitude toward Flick. Which lines suggest his feelings?

THE GUARD AT THE BINH THUY BRIDGE

How still he stands as mists begin to move,
as curling morning billows creep across

his cooplike, concrete sentry perched mid-bridge
over mid-muddy river. Stares at bush green banks
which bristle rifles, mortars, men—perhaps.   5
No convoys shake the timbers. No sound
but water slapping boat sides, bank sides, pilings.
He's slung his carbine barrel down to keep
the boring dry, and two banana-clips[1] instead of one
are taped to make, now, forty rounds instead   10
of twenty. Droplets bead from stock to sight;
they bulb, then strike his boot. He scrapes his heel,
and sees no box bombs floating towards his bridge.
Anchored in red morning mist a narrow junk
rocks its weight. A woman kneels on deck   15
staring at lapping water. Wets her face.
Idly the thick Rach[2] Binh Thuy slides by.
He aims. At her. Then drops his aim. Idly.

John Balaban

Questions and Comments

1. One element in a poem with a narrative structure is the field
   of vision which the poet grants the reader. Describe shifts in
   camera angle and distance which you would make in trans-
   lating this poem into film.

2. Besides being a "photographic study," this poem also makes
   a comment on American military involvement in Vietnam.
   Judging from the guard's actions, guess at his thoughts and
   feelings. Do you think he intended to fire at the woman on
   the junk? Explain your answer.

3. List the auditory images which the poet employs.

4. *M, n,* and *l* sounds continue when spoken, whereas *p, k,* and *t*
   sounds explode, disrupting the flow of sound. Note the
   clusters of continuants and explosives in the first three lines.

[1]*banana-clips:* the rifle's curved magazines
[2]*Rach:* Vietnamese word for *river*

99

There and in the remaining poem, sound patterns highlight the study in contrasting movements of river, mists, and soldier. Arrangement of lines and punctuation play their parts as well. Analyze this interplay of language and substance in some detail.

THE ARTIST

<pre>
Mr. T.
          bareheaded
                    in a soiled undershirt
his hair standing out
          on all sides   5
                    stood on his toes
heels together
          arms gracefully
                    for the moment
curled above his head.   10
                    Then he whirled about
                              bounded
into the air
          and with an *entrechat*[1]
                    perfectly achieved   15
completed the figure.
          My mother
                    taken by surprise
where she sat
          in her invalid's chair   20
                    was left speechless.
Bravo! she cried at last
          and clapped her hands.
                    The man's wife
</pre>

[1]*entrechat:* a ballet movement in which one leaps up and crosses one's legs several times in the air

came from the kitchen:
>What goes on here? she said.
>>But the show was over.

William Carlos Williams

Questions and Comments

1. From the characterization in the poem what can you guess of the circumstances of Mr. T's life? What evidence does Mrs. T's "What goes on here?" provide?

2. How does the mother's being in a wheelchair lend impact to the performance?

3. You may have inferred that Mr. T is not a dancer. Explain, then, the appropriateness of the poem's title.

4. What does the poem's shape on the page communicate?

ETCHING

No more than these: one act, one phrase,
Yet have they haunted all my days.

He wearied into the grocery store,
Slumped by the big stove's open door,

Plucked from the fire a graying coal   5
And, trembling it over his briar's bowl,

Lit up, then tossed it in the hod
Sighing despairingly, "My God!"

The calloused finger, calloused thumb
Holding a live coal, struck me dumb;   10

But deeper callous in his look,
And voice that darkened as it shook,

Made goose flesh on my spirit stand,
With living death so near at hand.

Wilbert Snow

Questions and Comments

1. What was the "act" referred to in line 1? The "phrase"? How does the title of the poem suggest the impact which the experience had on the speaker?

2. The word *haunted* in line 2 suggests unreality and ghostliness. What other words and phrases support this suggestion?

3. How is the word *calloused* used in line 9? How is the word *callous* used in line 11?

4. Cite the appeals to the sense of touch or muscular movement which the poem makes. Do you think they are appropriate? Why or why not?

FATHER WILLIAM

"You are old, Father William," the young man said,
 "And your hair has become very white;
And yet you incessantly stand on your head—
 Do you think, at your age, it is right?"

"In my youth," Father William replied to his son,   5
 "I feared it might injure the brain;
But, now that I'm perfectly sure I have none,
 Why, I do it again and again."

"You are old," said the youth, "as I mentioned before,
    And have grown most uncommonly fat;   10
Yet you turned a back-somersault in at the door—
    Pray, what is the reason of that?"

"In my youth," said the sage, as he shook his gray locks,
    "I kept all my limbs very supple
By the use of this ointment—one shilling the box—   15
    Allow me to sell you a couple?"

"You are old," said the youth, "and your jaws are too weak
    For anything tougher than suet;
Yet you finished the goose, with the bones and the beak—
    Pray, how did you manage to do it?"   20

"In my youth," said his father, "I took to the law,
    And argued each case with my wife;
And the muscular strength which it gave to my jaw
    Has lasted the rest of my life."

"You are old," said the youth, "one would hardly suppose 25
    That your eye was as steady as ever;
Yet you balanced an eel on the end of your nose—
    What made you so awfully clever?"

"I have answered three questions, and that is enough,"
    Said his father. "Don't give yourself airs!   30
Do you think I can listen all day to such stuff?
    Be off, or I'll kick you down-stairs!"

                                            Lewis Carroll

Questions and Comments

Much of the value of this poem comes from the fun it makes
of an earlier poem by Robert Southey, "The Old Man's Com-

forts and How He Gained Them," which opens with these two stanzas:

> "You are old, Father William," the young man cried;
>   "The few locks which are left you are gray;
> You are hale, Father William,—a hearty old man:
>   Now tell me the reason, I pray."
>
> "In the days of my youth," Father William replied,
>   "I remembered that youth would fly fast,
> And abused not my health and my vigor at first,
>   That I never might need them at last."

The Southey poem goes on for another four stanzas to moralize that the old man's optimism and spiritual serenity derive from his wisely spent youth.

1. In "Father William" what traits of the old man does the youth ask about?

2. What do Father William's responses reveal about the manner in which he prepared for the future?

3. What seems to be Carroll's attitude toward the relationship between youth and age as compared to Southey's (using the two stanzas shown and the comment above)?

MR. FLOOD'S PARTY

Old Eben Flood, climbing alone one night
Over the hill between the town below
And the forsaken upland hermitage
That held as much as he should ever know
On earth again of home, paused warily.   5
The road was his with not a native near;
And Eben, having leisure, said aloud,
For no man else in Tilbury Town to hear:

"Well, Mr. Flood, we have the harvest moon
Again, and we may not have many more;   10
The bird is on the wing,[1] the poet says,
And you and I have said it here before.
Drink to the bird." He raised up to the light
The jug that he had gone so far to fill,
And answered huskily: "Well, Mr. Flood,   15
Since you propose it, I believe I will."

Alone, as if enduring to the end
A valiant armor of scarred hopes outworn,
He stood there in the middle of the road
Like Roland's ghost[2] winding a silent horn.   20
Below him, in the town among the trees,
Where friends of other days had honored him,
A phantom salutation of the dead
Rang thinly till old Eben's eyes were dim.

Then, as a mother lays her sleeping child   25
Down tenderly, fearing it may awake,
He set the jug down slowly at his feet
With trembling care, knowing that most things break;
And only when assured that on firm earth
It stood, as the uncertain lives of men   30
Assuredly did not, he paced away,
And with his hand extended paused again:

"Well, Mr. Flood, we have not met like this
In a long time; and many a change has come
To both of us, I fear, since last it was   35
We had a drop together. Welcome home!"
Convivially returning with himself,

[1]*The Bird . . . wing:* a line from Edward Fitzgerald's poem, *The Rubaiyat of Omar Khayyam:* "The Bird of Time has but a little way/To flutter—and the Bird is on the wing."

[2]*Roland's ghost:* Roland was a legendary officer of Charlemagne. When attacked by a band of Saracens, he refused to blow his horn for aid until he was gravely wounded. Then he blew so hard that he died.

Again he raised the jug up to the light;
And with an acquisecent quaver said:
"Well, Mr. Flood, if you insist, I might.   40

"Only a very little, Mr. Flood—
For auld lang syne. No more, sir; that will do."
So, for the time, apparently it did,
And Eben evidently thought so too;
For soon amid the silver loneliness   45
Of night he lifted up his voice and sang,
Secure, with only two moons listening,
Until the whole harmonious landscape rang—

"For auld lang syne." The weary throat gave out,
The last word wavered, and the song was done.   50
He raised again the jug regretfully
And shook his head, and was again alone.
There was not much that was ahead of him,
And there was nothing in the town below—
Where strangers would have shut the many doors   55
That many friends had opened long ago.

                    Edwin Arlington Robinson

Questions and Comments

1. This poem is a kind of dramatic monologue, with stage directions and commentary. What is the scene of the drama? What
   is the situation as presented in the first sentence?

2. Explain the comparison in lines 17 and 18. How is the comparison developed and enriched by reference to Roland in
   line 20?

3. Account for Mr. Flood's loneliness. Do you feel that he has
   discredited himself with the townspeople because of his ex-
   cessive drinking, or do you feel that most of his friends are

dead? Support your answer to this question with evidence from the poem.

4. If you read "Eben Flood" as "ebb and flood," what significance is added to the name of the character? The "Eben Flood" of what . . . ?

5. What feelings for Mr. Flood do you think the poet has?

6. How is this picture of an older person different in manner and feeling from that in Wilbert Snow's "Etching" and that in Lewis Carroll's "Father William"?

RICHARD CORY

Whenever Richard Cory went down town,
We people on the pavement looked at him:
He was a gentleman from sole to crown,
Clean favored, and imperially slim.

And he was always quietly arrayed,   5
And he was always human when he talked;
But still he fluttered pulses when he said,
"Good-morning," and he glittered when he walked.

And he was rich—yes, richer than a king—
And admirably schooled in every grace: 10
In fine,[1] we thought that he was everything
To make us wish that we were in his place.

So on we worked, and waited for the light,
And went without the meat, and cursed the bread;
And Richard Cory, one calm summer night,   15
Went home and put a bullet through his head.

Edwin Arlington Robinson

[1] *In fine:* in conclusion

Questions and Comments

1. The characterizations of Richard Cory and of the towns-people, represented by the speaker, contrast. What words and phrases show what the townspeople consider attributes of royalty and gentility? In what respects are the townspeople different from Richard Cory? How does the speaker's description of Richard Cory serve to characterize the townspeople? (The word *but* introducing line 7 is significant.)

2. What does the word *light* (line 13) mean to you?

3. What indications does the poet give us of what Richard Cory is really like? The name Cory suggests "core," the heart of any matter. Is Richard's core hard or soft? Troubled or serene? What contrast does "one calm summer night" (line 15) suggest to you?

4. One definition of *irony* is the contrast between the actual outcome of a series of events and the ending one would normally expect. Would you call this poem "ironic"? Explain your answer.

nobody loses all the time

nobody loses all the time

i had an uncle named
Sol who was a born failure and
nearly everybody said he should have gone
into vaudeville perhaps because my Uncle Sol could   5
sing McCann He Was A Diver on Xmas Eve like Hell Itself
    which
may or may not account for the fact that my Uncle

Sol indulged in that possibly most inexcusable
of all to use a highfalootin phrase

luxuries that is or to
wit farming and be
it needlessly
added

10

my Uncle Sol's farm
failed because the chickens
ate the vegetables so
my Uncle Sol had a
chicken farm till the
skunks ate the chickens when

15

my Uncle Sol
had a skunk farm but
the skunks caught cold and
died and so
my Uncle Sol imitated the
skunks in a subtle manner

20

25

or by drowning himself in the watertank
but somebody who'd given my Uncle Sol a Victor
Victrola and records while he lived presented to
him upon the auspicious occasion of his decease a
scrumptious not to mention splendiferous funeral with
tall boys in black gloves and flowers and everything and

30

i remember we all cried like the Missouri
when my Uncle Sol's coffin lurched because
somebody pressed a button
(and down went
my Uncle
Sol

35

and started a worm farm)

e. e. cummings

Questions and Comments

1. On the basis of the details which we get concerning Uncle Sol, what do you think might be the speaker's definition of success? Why do you suppose the speaker regards farming as a luxury? Account for the connection between vaudeville and farming in the speaker's mind. The first line suggests that the speaker thinks Uncle Sol gained something at a certain point. What is it that Uncle Sol is thought to have gained?

2. Although he was a failure according to some people's standards, would you say Uncle Sol played a significant role in nature's scheme of things?

3. What are some of the symbols of material affluence in the poem? At certain points, like the description of the funeral, does the speaker's choice of words and expressions strike you as pretentious? Point out these words and phrases. How might these be clues to the speaker's set of values?

4. Like Richard Cory, Uncle Sol committed suicide. Why do you think each man ended his life?

THE UNKNOWN CITIZEN

(To JS/07/M/378
This Marble Monument
Is Erected by the State)

He was found by the Bureau of Statistics to be
One against whom there was no official complaint,
And all the reports on his conduct agree
That, in the modern sense of an old-fashioned word, he
    was a saint,
For in everything he did he served the Greater
    Community,   5
Except for the War till the day he retired
He worked in a factory and never got fired,

But satisfied his employers, Fudge Motors Inc.
Yet he wasn't a scab[1] or odd in his views,
For his Union reports that he paid his dues, 10
(Our report on his Union shows it was sound)
And our Social Psychology workers found
That he was popular with his mates and liked a drink.
The Press was convinced that he bought a paper every
    day
And that his reactions to advertisements were normal
    in every way. 15
Policies taken out in his name prove that he was fully
    insured,
And his Health-card shows he was once in the hospital
    but left it cured.
Both Producers Research and High-Grade Living
    declare
He was fully sensible to the advantages of the
    Installment Plan
And had everything necessary to the Modern Man, 20
A phonograph, a radio, a car and a frigidaire.
Our researchers into Public Opinion are content
That he held the proper opinions for the time of year;
When there was peace, he was for peace; when there
    was war, he went.
He was married and added five children to the
    population, 25
Which our Eugenist[2] says was the right number for a
    parent of his generation,
And our teachers report that he never interfered with
    their education.
Was he free? Was he happy? The question is absurd:
Had anything been wrong, we should certainly have
    heard.

W. H. Auden

[1]*scab:* one who refuses to join a labor union
[2]*Eugenist:* specialist in the genetic improvement of the human species
by controlled breeding

Questions and Comments

1. Identify the "we" who tell about JS/07/M/378. What seem to be their standards of good citizenship?

2. The Unknown Solider of our country was so called because his remains were unidentifiable. With the mass of statistical information available, how is this citizen still "unknown"? To what extent was he a recognizable individual?

3. What kind of citizen does JS/07/M/378 strike you as having been?

4. Might some of the goods and services distributed by the state discourage independent achievement? Explain your answer.

5. If a citizen of a state is depersonalized, whose fault is it? What are some characteristics of good citizenship which Auden himself seems to value? Comment on the educational values of "interfering" with your teacher's strategy.

Composition

1. Write thumbnail sketches of the following characters, sketches which might have appeared in their high-school yearbooks: Gert Swasey, Flick Webb, Richard Corey, Uncle Sol, and the Unknown Citizen.

2. Does one of the portraits in the preceding section of poems remind you of a character in your town or city? Write a sketch of that person in which you try to do justice to what you regard as his or her memorable characteristics.

3. With reference to "I'm Nobody! Who Are You?" write a composition in which you present some of the disadvantages which go along with being famous.

4. This gallery of portraits is filled with people who had trouble "making it." Discuss the proposition that failure is more interesting than success.

5. With reference to David Wagoner's "Every Good Boy Does Fine," what embarrassing experience have you had which would match those in the poem? Relate this experience.

6. Writing on the subject with which "Father William" is concerned, Henry David Thoreau in *Walden* seriously questions the value of the advice that older people can give. He writes as follows: "What old people say you cannot do you try and find that you can. Old deeds for old people, and new deeds for new. . . . Age is no better, hardly so well, qualified for an instructor as youth, for it has not profited so much as it has lost. One may almost doubt if the wisest man has learned anything of absolute value by living. Practically, the old have no very important advice to give the young. . . . I have lived some thirty years on this planet, and I have yet to hear the first syllable of valuable or even earnest advice from my seniors." Discuss the validity of this statement in terms of your own experience.

7. Find a reproduction of a painting, such as the Mona Lisa, or a photograph, such as you might find in Edward Steichen's *The Family of Man,* and write a word sketch of the subject based upon your observation of the picture.

8. Which poem in this section made the most favorable impression upon you? Which made the least favorable impression? Give reasons for your choices.

9. Compare "nobody loses all the time" with "Richard Cory" in such matters as main character, speaker, and manner in which the story is told.

PROBLEMS OF HUMANITY

Along with problems of growing up and problems of love, there are other human problems, several of which are suggested by the poems in this section. These poems depict for us deserts of loneliness and jungles of dilemma; at the same time, they speak in their various voices of the certainty of responsibility and of the importance of courage.

THE MERRY-GO-ROUND

JARDIN DU LUXEMBOURG

Under the roof and the roof's shadow turns
this train of painted horses for a while
in this bright land that lingers
before it perishes. In what brave style
they prance—though some pull wagons.   5
And there burns
a wicked lion red with anger...

and now and then a big white elephant.

Even a stag runs here, as in the wood,
save that he bears a saddle where, upright,   10
a little girl in blue sits, buckled tight.

And on the lion whitely rides a young
boy who clings with little sweaty hands,
the while the lion shows his teeth and tongue.

And now and then a big white elephant.   15

And on the horses swiftly going by
are shining girls who have outgrown this play;
in the middle of the flight they let their eyes
glance here and there and near and far away—

and now and then a big white elephant.   20

And all this hurries toward the end, so fast,
whirling futilely, evermore the same.
A flash of red, of green, of gray, goes past,
and then a little scarce-begun profile.
And oftentimes a blissful dazzling smile   25
vanishes in this blind and breathless game.

Rainer Maria Rilke

Questions and Comments

1. Which words and phrases suggest a "merry-go-round" movement? How is the structure of the poem appropriate to its subject?

2. Comment on Rilke's sketching of several riders. Are the reactions of the shining girls to their ride different from those of the young children? Explain your answer.

3. Recast the sense of lines 2, 3, and 4 in your own words. Relate this statement to that of the final stanza. Which words imply a particular attitude on the part of the speaker?

4. How might the mechanical merry-go-round be a symbol of life beyond the amusement park?

CONFLICT

The sea is forever quivering,
The shore forever still;
And the boy who is born in a seacoast town
Is born with a dual will:
The sunburned rocks and beaches
Inveigle him to stay;
While every wave that breaches
Is a nudge to be up and away.

Wilbert Snow

Questions and Comments

1. What is the conflict that the poet speaks about? What visual images in the poem help to depict the conflict?

2. Which elements in the poem portray adventure? Which portray security? Did you note a similar conflict between adventure and security in "Travel"? Which impulse seems to win out in that poem? Which impulse seems to win out in this poem? Explain your answer.

3. Look up the words *inveigle* (line 6) and *breaches* (line 7). These verbs represent the action of the two forces which contribute to the boy's conflict. Do you detect a tone of treachery in their calls? If so, is this tone justified in terms of your view of life?

INCIDENT

Once riding in old Baltimore,
    Heart-filled, head-filled with glee,
I saw a Baltimorean
    Keep looking straight at me.

Now I was eight and very small,   5
    And he was no whit bigger,
And so I smiled, but he poked out
    His tongue, and called me, "Nigger."

I saw the whole of Baltimore
    From May until December;   10
Of all the things that happened there
    That's all that I remember.

Countee Cullen

Questions and Comments

1. What is the function of each stanza in the development of the main idea of this poem?

2. What seem to have been the young visitor's attitudes toward racial difference prior to the encounter? After the encounter? What evidence is there in the poem to support your view?

3. What feelings do you have in reaction to this poem? Which elements in the situation promote these feelings?

ELDORADO

Gaily bedight,[1]
A gallant knight,
In sunshine and in shadow,

[1] *bedight:* arrayed, decked out

Had journeyed long,
Singing a song,
In search of Eldorado.[1]   5

But he grew old—
This knight so bold—
And o'er his heart a shadow
    Fell as he found   10
    No spot of ground
That looked like Eldorado.

And, as his strength
Failed him at length,
He met a pilgrim shadow—   15
    "Shadow," said he,
    "Where can it be—
This land of Eldorado?"

"Over the Mountains
    Of the Moon,   20
Down the Valley of the Shadow,
    Ride, boldly ride,"
    The shade replied,—
"If you seek for Eldorado!"

Edgar Allan Poe

Questions and Comments

1. Do you consider the Knight as a universal representative of humanity or as merely a particular type of person?

2. What does the action of the poem imply about the quest for the ideal?

3. Poe uses the word *shadow* in each stanza. Trace the word's changes in meaning in its successive contexts. Explain the allusion: "The Valley of the Shadow."

[1]*Eldorado:* an imaginary kingdom abounding in gold

BOTH SIDES NOW

Bows and flows of angel hair,
And ice-cream castles in the air,
And feather canyons everywhere,
I've looked at clouds that way.
But now they only block the sun,   5
They rain and snow on everyone,
So many things I would have done,
But clouds got in my way.
   I've looked at clouds from both sides now
   From up and down, and still somehow   10
   It's cloud illusions I recall;
   I really don't know clouds at all.

Moons and tunes and ferris wheels,
The dizzy dancing way you feel
When every fairytale comes real,   15
I've looked at love that way.
But now it's just another show,
You leave 'em laughin' when you go.
And if you care, don't let them know,
Don't give yourself away.   20
   I've looked at love from both sides now,
   From give and take, and still somehow
   It's love's illusions I recall;
   I really don't know love at all.

Tears and fears and feelin' proud   25
To say I love you right out loud,
Dreams and schemes and circus crowds,
I've looked at life that way.
But now old friends are acting strange,
They shake their heads, they say I've changed,   30
Well, something's lost but something's gained
In living every day.

I've looked at life from both sides now,
From win and lose, and still somehow
It's life's illusions I recall;   35
I really don't know life at all.

Joni Mitchell

Questions and Comments

1. *Structure* may be defined as the order and relationship among the parts of a poem. Name the subject of each stanza and comment on any progression you note in the poem's structure. How do the images of each stanza reflect a different stage of life?

2. A second aspect of structure is the relationship of elements *within* stanzas. How many lines are devoted to the bright side of things? To the dark side? Do the indented final four lines of each stanza balance good and bad, or do they tip the scales in one direction or another? Explain your reasoning.

3. What is the speaker's attitude toward illusion in life? Toward harsher experience?

4. Compare the theme (or ideas) and structure of "Both Sides Now" with those of Countee Cullen's "Incident," and with those of Poe's "Eldorado."

TIRED AND UNHAPPY,
YOU THINK OF HOUSES

Tired and unhappy, you think of houses
Soft-carpeted and warm in the December evening,
While snow's white pieces fall past the window,
And the orange firelight leaps.

A young girl sings   5
That song of Gluck[1] where Orpheus pleads with Death;
Her elders watch, nodding their happiness
To see time fresh again in her self-conscious eyes:
The servants bring the coffee, the children retire,
Elder and younger yawn and go to bed,   10
The coals fade and glow, rose and ashen,
It is time to shake yourself! and break this
Banal dream, and turn your head
Where the underground is charged, where the weight
Of the lean buildings is seen,   15
Where close in the subway rush, anonymous
In the audience, well-dressed or mean,
So many surround you, ringing your fate,
Caught in an anger exact as a machine!

Delmore Schwartz

Questions and Comments

1. Half the poem is an imagined scene—or dream scene. Where does the dream begin? Where does it end? What words signal the shift from dream to reality?

2. In what ways does the imagined scene differ from the actual one? What is the mood or atmosphere of each scene? How do you relate the scene of Gluck's opera to the setting in which the speaker wakes?

3. In which scene do we receive the more vivid impression of people? Are the people in the dream scene really different from those in the subway, or are they different in the speaker's perception?

---

[1] *Gluck:* an 18th century German composer. A central scene in his opera *Orfeo* is that in which Orpheus goes to the lower regions to beg Pluto to return his dead young wife, Eurydice, to earth.

4. What is the effect of the dreamer's depicting both young and old members of a family in the presence of a gradually sinking fire?

5. In the last section of the poem are several words calculated to give the reader a sense of captivity or restricted movement. What are these words and phrases? What possible meanings does the phrase "ringing your fate" suggest to you?

DUST OF SNOW

The way a crow
Shook down on me
The dust of snow
From a hemlock tree

Has given my heart
A change of mood
And saved some part
Of a day I had rued.

Robert Frost

Questions and Comments

1. What general impression do you have of the speaker? In your own words, account for the speaker's change in mood.

2. In which of the two stanzas are the concrete images more numerous? What contrasts do you find in the poem?

3. What associations do you have with the word *crow*? The word *dust*? The word *hemlock*? In light of those associations, comment on the poet's use of the word *saved*.

4. Do you detect any irony in this poem? Explain your answer.

122

INCIDENT OF THE COAST

One cold December morning—crackling cold,
The metal waters of Penobscot Bay[1]
Curled into vapor on the zero air,
When Harry, rising from his bed to haul,[2]
Said, "Brrr, it's bitter, bet my mittens freeze   5
Stiff between each pot out there in the bay."

His young wife, starting coffee, begged in vain,
"Harry, leave your boat stay on the mooring."

Into the cold he went: he heard a board
Burst from a nail on the barn as he went by;   10
He felt a hardness in the path that met
His rubber boots with stubborn enmity;
He saw a poplar shivering in the air
Where no wind was; dragged, over delicate ice,
His tender to the motorboat; far off   15
Saw vapor rising like a pillar of cloud
Over the bay; then, hesitant, stooped down,
Turned on his gas, drained twice his priming cup,
Spun round and round the wheel, and left the cove.
An hour's run, he made his outmost trap,   20
And gaffed[3] the buoy, floating white and red,
The red sparkling with frost, the white lit up
With ruddy streaks out of the eastern sky,
As sunrise flaming through the cold air turned
The bay to a crater bright enough to catch   25
Indifferent eyes and hold them with its roll
And flow of streaming wine-drip over the sea.

[1]*Penobscot Bay:* an inlet at the mouth of the Penobscot River in Maine.
[2]*haul:* to take in the lobster traps which are full
[3]*gaffed:* hooked

In his eyes no indifference: he saw
Too well the play of tint on tint, awe-struck
At all the panorama of the morning: 30
Ultramarine above, gun-barrel blue
Along the bleak horizon, while around
The red cliffs of the islands weird mirages
Blurred the fixed lines of distance over the bay
Till they went antigodlin[1] everywhere,   35
Like northern lights across an Arctic sky.
Mechanically he took the counters[2] out,
Baited his trap, and, heedless, threw it over,
His mind preoccupied with loveliness;
Started his engine dreamily, then woke   40
To find the tangled warp had twisted round
The whirling shaft and blades of his propeller,
So tightly drawn the flywheel would not budge.

White scuds were rising in the northwest now,
A breeze was ruffling green and white the bay.   45
He felt the woolen mittens on his hands
Stiffen with ice; alarmingly he felt
His body stiffen, and lean hounds of cold
With snapping teeth jab at his whitened skin.
"I'm going for it," he cried out, recalling   50
Long-forgotten tales of freezing men.
Desperate, he grabbed a cod line, threw it over,
Relayed it in, and threw it out again,
Till eighty times had set his young blood stirring.

---

[1] *antigodlin:* askew (used chiefly in Midland United States). The poet
writes, "I never heard the word *antigodlin* but once. But it fascinated me.
An old man was talking to another old man about the boundaries of a piece
of property in the woods. The boundaries were not laid out with exactitude.
The way he talked about them they seemed to be running every which way.
So when I went to describe the blurred lines of distance on a vapor-scattered
sea I thought of the old man and used the word."
[2] *counters:* lobsters of the prescribed legal length

His hands grew warm, his mittens limp. He tried   55
Pulling the warp out with his gaff, but made
No headway—and the north wind piping on.

Death tightened on that warp and challenged him.
He knew no rescue boat would come; he heard
Death's mockery snarling on the icy wind,   60
And met the challenge. Stripping off his clothes,
Stark naked, with a splitting knife in hand,
He plunged in the wintry waters, swimming down
Under the stern, where he slashed and pulled away
The deadly warp, till, at the last frayed end   65
Of the warp that bound him to the trap of life,
He tumbled over the side, teeth chattering, numb,
Hauled on his clothes, and headed for the harbor.

Down, to the ice-caked shore the neighbors came,
Watching his wherry push the waves apart.   70
Laden with layers of ice, caught from the spray
And held in all its dazzling glitter fast
Upon the washboards, low on the waves she sagged;
And when he pulled his switch, men clambered down,
Steadied his feet, faltering on frozen seaweed,   75
And moored his craft, while he went stumbling home.

Wilbert Snow

Questions and Comments

"Incident of the Coast" is one of the few narrative poems in this book. You should read it with an eye to the development of character, setting, and plot, as you would read a short story.

1. What function do lines 2-4 serve in the narrative? Lines 21-36?

2. What quality in the lobster trapper's character leads to the act which nearly cost him his life?

3. Explain the metaphor in lines 48 and 49.

4. To which of your senses do lines 52-55 appeal?

5. How do lines 58-61 relate to the action of the narrative? What meanings do you get from "the trap of life" (line 66)?

6. What is the climax of the action in the poem? Explain your answer.

7. What function does the last stanza of the narrative serve?

THE GREY SQUIRREL

Like a small grey
coffee-pot
sits the squirrel.
He is not

all he should be,   5
kills by dozens
trees, and eats
his red-brown cousins.

The keeper, on the
other hand   10
,who shot him, is
a Christian, and

loves his enemies,
which shows
the squirrel was not   15
one of those.

Humbert Wolfe

Questions and Comments

1. To what does the poet compare the squirrel in lines 1 and 2? What sort of associations does this metaphor arouse in you? What contrast do you detect between the imagery of the second stanza and that of lines 1 and 2?

2. Why do you think the poet chose to say "is not all he should be" rather than to use stronger language? Who are the grey squirrel's "red-brown cousins"?

3. Who is the "keeper"? What associations do you have in response to the word *keeper*? Why does the poet make the point that he is a Christian? State the idea which you think the poet wants to suggest to us.

4. What reason can you think of for the surprising placement of the first comma in line 11?

5. Which lines rhyme? The rhyme is especially muted in the first and third stanzas because the final rhyming words are not usually stressed in conversational patterns and also because the final lines of these stanzas are nonstop, ending in the middle of sense units.

THE FISH

I caught a tremendous fish
and held him beside the boat
half out of water, with my hook
fast in a corner of his mouth.
He didn't fight.   5
He hadn't fought at all.
He hung a grunting weight,
battered and venerable
and homely. Here and there
his brown skin hung in strips   10
like ancient wall-paper,

and its pattern of darker brown
was like wall-paper:
shapes like full-blown roses
stained and lost through age. 15
He was speckled with barnacles,
fine rosettes of lime,
and infested
with tiny white sea-lice,
and underneath two or three 20
rags of green weed hung down.
While his gills were breathing in
the terrible oxygen
—the frightening gills,
fresh and crisp with blood, 25
that can cut so badly—
I thought of the coarse white flesh
packed in like feathers,
the big bones and the little bones,
the dramatic reds and blacks 30
of his shiny entrails,
and the pink swim-bladder
like a big peony.
I looked into his eyes
which were far larger than mine 35
but shallower, and yellowed,
the irises backed and packed
with tarnished tinfoil
seen through the lenses
of old scratched isinglass. 40
They shifted a little, but not
to return my stare.
—It was more like the tipping
of an object toward the light.
I admired his sullen face, 45
the mechanism of his jaw,
and then I saw
that from his lower lip

—if you could call it a lip—
grim, wet, and weapon-like,   50
hung five old pieces of fish-line,
or four and a wire leader
with the swivel still attached,
with all their five big hooks
grown firmly in his mouth.   55
A green line, frayed at the end
where he broke it, two heavier lines,
and a fine black thread
still crimped from the strain and snap
when it broke and he got away.   60
Like medals with their ribbons
frayed and wavering,
a five-haired beard of wisdom
trailing from his aching jaw.
I stared and stared   65
and victory filled up
the little rented boat,
from the pool of bilge
where oil had spread a rainbow
around the rusted engine   70
to the bailer rusted orange,
the sun-cracked thwarts,[1]
the oarlocks on their strings,
the gunnels[2]—until everything
was rainbow, rainbow, rainbow!   75
And I let the fish go.

Elizabeth Bishop

Questions and Comments

1. What details used by the poet in the description of the fish
   do you find to be particularly vivid? What objects or materials

[1] *thwarts:* narrow seats or cross-braces
[2] *gunnels:* gunwales, the rim forming the frame for the sides of the boat

129

not normally associated with fish does the poet use to sharpen the visual images we receive? (If you found fewer than six, read the poem again with an eye to the stated and implied comparisons.) How do these comparisons help to create our sense of the speaker's attitude toward the fish? Describe that attitude in your own words.

2. To what are the five hooks and fish lines in the fish's "aching jaw" compared? What feelings for the fish do these comparisons suggest?

3. With which words does the poet seem to attribute a particular attitude to the fish—an attitude toward being hooked? Why do you think the fish "hadn't fought at all"? How do you reconcile this fact with the details given in lines 48-61?

4. What is the "victory" mentioned in line 66? Why do you think the speaker let the fish go? Consider lines 65-75 in your answer.

5. Do you find any similarity in the ideas suggested by this poem and those suggested by "The Grey Squirrel"? Explain your answer.

TRAVELING THROUGH THE DARK

Traveling through the dark I found a deer
dead on the edge of the Wilson River road.
It is usually best to roll them into the canyon:
that road is narrow; to swerve might make more dead.

By glow of the tail-light I stumbled back of the car   5
and stood by the heap, a doe, a recent killing;
she had stiffened already, almost cold.
I dragged her off; she was large in the belly.

My fingers touching her side brought me the reason—
her side was warm; her fawn lay there waiting,   10

130

alive, still, never to be born.
Beside that mountain road I hesitated.

The car aimed ahead its lowered parking lights;
under the hood purred the steady engine.
I stood in the glare of the warm exhaust turning red;   15
around our group I could hear the wilderness listen.

I thought hard for us all—my only swerving—
then I pushed her over the edge into the river.

William Stafford

Questions and Comments

1. In the simple.and direct statement of the poem, the word
   choice in line 16 ("around our group I could hear the wilderness listen") stands out. What effects derive from the words
   "our group"? From the representation of a "listening
   wilderness"?

2. Trace the course of what might have been the reasoning
   which led the speaker to push the dead doe into the river.

3. Comment on the use of the verb "swerve" in line 4 and again
   in line 17.

4. How does Stafford help us experience the decision facing his
   speaker? Might some of this effect come from his "non-poetic"
   style—irregular pattern of stresses with a barely discernible
   rhyme scheme (lines 2 and 4, 6 and 8, etc.)? Explain your
   reasoning.

COME UP FROM THE FIELDS FATHER

Come up from the fields father, here's a letter from our Pete,
And come to the front door mother, here's a letter from thy
  dear son.

Lo, 't is autumn,

Lo, where the trees, deeper green, yellower and redder,

Cool and sweeten Ohio's villages with leaves fluttering in the
moderate wind,   5

Where apples ripe in the orchards hang and grapes on the
trellis'd vines,

(Smell you the smell of the grapes on the vines?

Smell you the buckwheat where the bees were lately buzz-
ing?)

Above all, lo, the sky so calm, so transparent after the rain,
and with wondrous clouds,

Below too, all calm, all vital and beautiful, and the farm
prospers well.   10

Down in the fields all prospers well,

But now from the fields come father, come at the daughter's
call.

And come to the entry mother, to the front door come right
away.

Fast as she can she hurries, something ominous, her steps
trembling,

She does not tarry to smooth her hair nor adjust her cap.   15

Open the envelope quickly,

O this is not our son's writing, yet his name is sign'd,

O a strange hand writes for our dear son, O stricken mother's
soul!

All swims before her eyes, flashes with black, she catches the
main words only,

Sentences broken, *gunshot wound in the breast, cavalry skir-
mish, taken to hospital,*   20

At present low, but will soon be better.

Ah now the single figure to me,

132

Amid all teeming and wealthy Ohio with all its cities and farms,
Sickly white in the face and dull in the head, very faint,
By the jamb of a door leans.   25
Grieve not so, dear mother (the just-grown daughter speaks through her sobs,
The little sisters huddle around speechless and dismay'd),
See, dearest mother, the letter says Pete will soon be better.

Alas poor boy, he will never be better (nor may-be needs to be better, that brave and simple soul),
While they stand at home at the door he is dead already,   30
The only son is dead.

But the mother needs to be better,
She with thin form presently drest in black,
By day her meals untouch'd, then at night fitfully sleeping, often waking,
In the midnight waking, weeping, longing with one deep longing,   35

O that she might withdraw unnoticed, silent from life escape and withdraw,
To follow, to seek, to be with her dear dead son.

Walt Whitman

Questions and Comments

Although the reader can readily understand the action of this poem, one can become confused in trying to identify the several voices that speak in the poem. The poem is not, as the first line may lead you to believe, straight dialogue; neither is it objective description. Nor is it a conventional combination of the two devices. The problem may be solved to a great extent, however, if one sees the poem as uttered by one speaker, an invisible, all-seeing partner to the woes of this family. At certain points the speaker takes the parts of different members of the family in tones of immediate speech; at other points the reader seems to be directly spoken to. At other times the speaker is the sober, detached commentator. The author of this poem, Walt Whitman, lived during the Civil War, and he was harrowed by the agony of fellow Americans bearing arms against each other. Perhaps his identification with individuals and with the nation as a whole accounts for the fact that he speaks to us through several voices.

1. Which lines in the poem suggest that they might be the words of members of the family?

2. The central tragic event explodes in a peaceful setting. Which lines communicate the peacefulness?

3. Characterize the attitude of the speaker toward war. Which lines most vividly communicate these feelings in your view?

AUTO WRECK

Its quick soft silver bell beating, beating,
And down the dark one ruby flare
Pulsing out red like an artery,
The ambulance at top speed floating down
Past beacons and illuminated clocks   5
Wings in a heavy curve, dips down,
And brakes speed, entering the crowd.
The doors leap open, emptying light;
Stretchers are laid out, the mangled lifted
And stowed into the little hospital.   10
Then the bell, breaking the hush, tolls once,
And the ambulance with its terrible cargo
Rocking, slightly rocking, moves away,
As the doors, an afterthought, are closed.

We are deranged, walking among the cops   15
Who sweep glass and are large and composed.

One is still making notes under the light.
One with a bucket douches ponds of blood
Into the street and gutter.
One hangs lanterns on the wrecks that cling,   20
Empty husks of locusts, to iron poles.

Our throats were tight as tourniquets,
Our feet were bound with splints, but now,
Like convalescents intimate and gauche,
We speak through sickly smiles and warn   25
With the stubborn saw[1] of common sense,
The grim joke and the banal resolution.
The traffic moves around with care,
But we remain, touching a wound
That opens to our richest horror.   30

Already old, the question Who shall die?
Becomes unspoken Who is innocent?
For death in war is done by hands;
Suicide has cause and stillbirth, logic;
And cancer, simple as a flower, blooms.   35
But this invites the occult[2] mind,
Cancels our physics with a sneer,
And splatters all we knew of denouement[3]
Across the expedient and wicked stones.

Karl Shapiro

Questions and Comments

1. Which words and phrases in lines 1–14 appeal to the sense
of muscular movement? Explain the metaphor used by the

[1] *saw:* a saying or a maxim

[2] *occult:* concerned with magical powers of solving mysteries

[3] *denouement:* a conclusion growing out of a complex situation; a solution
which clarifies the action that has gone before it

poet in line 3. What word in line 12 is particularly related to *stowed* in line 10? Can you make any associations with the words "the bell . . . tolls" (line 11)? Explain.

2. What word in line 16 strikes a contrasting note to *deranged* in line 15? To what are "husks of locusts" (line 21) compared? Do you find this to be an appropriate metaphor? Explain your answer.

3. Do you find the metaphors in lines 22-24 effective? Explain your answer.

4. What commonsense sayings, jokes, and resolutions, as mentioned in lines 25-27, do people utter at times such as the one described in this poem?

5. The question "Who shall die?" (line 31) is usually pondered by survivors of death, but in cases of death by accident there follows an additional question, "Who was responsible?" What attitude on the speaker's part do you suppose has led to the rephrasing of this second question in line 32? To what does *this* (line 36) refer? What does the speaker say about death in war, by suicide, or from illness? About death in an auto accident? What is meant by the phrase "cancels our physics" (line 37)?

6. What are the stones mentioned in the final line? For whom are these stones "expedient"? Do you find that the poet's selection of the word *expedient* implies an answer to the question posed in line 32, "Who is innocent?" Explain.

7. What do you suppose was the poet's purpose in writing this poem? How does his purpose, as you see it, differ from that of a newspaper reporter with the assignment of covering an accident?

Composition

1. Write a news story based upon the event described in "Incident of the Coast."

2. Write an editorial, pro or con, on hunting as a sport.

3. With reference to Richard Wilbur's "Dust of Snow," describe a snow scene from your own life which holds particular significance for you.

4. Write a composition in which you discuss one or two problems which you have faced during the past two years which changed your outlook on life.

5. Write a composition in which you consider the idea that poets and novelists tell us more about the problems of humanity than do journalists and sociologists. You may agree or disagree with this idea.

6. The problems of humanity which this section treats are varied; nevertheless, try to classify each of the poems as it portrays a human being in conflict with (1) nature, (2) other human beings, or (3) self. In a composition, defend your classification of "Incident of the Coast," "Traveling Through the Dark," and "Auto Wreck."

DEATH IN LIFE

A last and very important problem that people face is death. We are mourners of death and finally its victims. When we must face it, we do so with the volume of our emotions turned all the way up. From one point of view, our concern with death is an index of our feeling for life; realizing that life must end quickens out appreciation for it.

One value of encountering death in poetry and in other works of literature is that it gives us a chance to think about it without becoming personally involved. We, especially the poets among us, are individually very much interested in these matters, as we are in the development of power and the accomplishment of high deeds, because the meeting of doom is part of life. To contemplate death objectively helps us live.

CRYSTAL MOMENT

Once or twice this side of death
Things can make one hold his breath.

From my boyhood I remember
A crystal moment of September.

A wooded island rang with sounds   5
Of church bells in the throats of hounds.

A buck leaped out and took the tide
With jewels flowing past each side.

With his high head like a tree
He swam within a yard of me.   10

I saw the golden drop of light
In his eyes turned dark with fright.

I saw the forest's holiness
On him like a fierce caress.

Fear made him lovely past belief,   15
My heart was trembling like a leaf.

He leaned towards the land and life
With need upon him like a knife.

In his wake the hot hounds churned,
They stretched their muzzles out and yearned. 20

They bayed no more, but swam and throbbed,
Hunger drove them till they sobbed.

Pursued, pursuers reached the shore
And vanished. I saw nothing more.

So they passed, a pageant such   25
As only gods could witness much,

Life and death upon one tether
And running beautiful together.

Robert P. Tristram Coffin

139

Questions and Comments

1. Note that each stanza is made up of two lines which rhyme. Two such rhymed lines are called a *couplet*. What function does the final couplet have?

2. Lines 5-18 contain a chain of rapid-fire comparisons. Point out some of them. Which do you find to be most effective? Why? Which do you find to be least effective? Why?

3. Why does the poet couple "land" and "life" (line 17)?

4. What is the poet suggesting in lines 13 and 14? Would you see beauty in a frightened animal? Why or why not? Is this the same sort of reaction Robert Frost voices in "The Runaway"? Explain your answer.

5. Why does this experience have such an impact upon the poet? What is the relationship between lines 13 and 14 and the final four lines of the poem? What is the relationship of the title and the final couplet? What is meant by "Life and death upon one tether"?

OLD CHRISTMAS

"Where you coming from, Lomey[1] Carter,
    So early over the snow?
What's them pretties you got in your hand,
    And where you aiming to go?

Step in, Honey. Old Christmas morning   5
    We hain't got nothing much;
Maybe a bite of sweetness and corn bread,
    A little ham meat and such.

But come in, Lomey. Sally Ann Barton's
    Hungering after your face.   10

---

[1] *Lomey:* probably from the woman's name, Salome

140

Wait till I light my candle up.
   Set down. There's your old place.

Where you been, so early this morning?"
   "Graveyard, Sally Ann:
Up by the trace[1] in the Salt Lick meadow   15
   Where Taulbe kilt my man."

"Taulbe hain't to home this morning.
   Wisht I could scratch me a light:
Dampness gits in the heads of the matches;
   I'll blow up my embers bright."   20

"Needn't trouble. I won't be stopping:
   Going a long way still."
"You didn't see nothing, Lomey Carter,
   Up on the graveyard hill?"

"What should I see there, Sally Ann Barton?"   25
   "Spirits walk loose[2] last night."
"There was an elder bush a blooming
   While the moon still give some light."

"Yes, elder bushes they bloom, Old Christmas,
   And critters kneel down in their straw.   30
Anything else? Up in the graveyard?"
   "One thing more I saw:

I saw my man with his head all bleeding
   Where Taulbe's shot went through."
"What did he say?" "He stooped and kissed me."   35
   "What did he say to you?"

"Said Lord Jesus forgive your Taulbe;
   But he told me another word;
Said it soft when he stooped and kissed me;
   That was the last I heard."   40

[1] *trace:* path   [2] *walk loose:* re-enter their earthly forms and move about

"Taulbe hain't come home this morning."
  "I know that, Sally Ann,
For I kilt him, coming down through the meadow
  Where Taulbe kilt my man.

I met him up on the meadow trace   45
  When the moon was fainting fast;
I had my dead man's rifle gun,
  And kilt him as he come past."

"I heard two shots." " 'Twas his was second:
  He got me 'fore he died.   50
You'll find us at daybreak, Sally Ann Barton:
  I'm laying there dead at his side."

                              Roy Helton

Questions and Comments

This poem is called a *literary ballad* because it was written by one person. "Lord Randal" and "Flora, the Lily of the West" are called *folk ballads* because their compositions were cooperative, taking place over a long period of time. Of course, the writer of the literary ballad usually follows the conventions of the older form and tries to invest a work with the old flavor. Notice the ways in which "Old Christmas" adheres to the folk tradition.

Old Christmas is January 6, formerly the day on which Christmas was celebrated, now called Epiphany. According to Kentucky mountain superstition, on Old Christmas Eve animals kneel to pray, elder trees blossom, and dead people walk the earth.

1. What does the third stanza suggest about the background of this drama? What do you guess about the relationships of the men and the women prior to the shooting of Carter?

2. At what point does Lomey Carter speak for the first time?

3. To what do you suppose the phrase "them pretties" (line 3) refers? What do you suppose the other "word" (line 38) might have been?

4. Characterize the two women who speak. What evidence is there in the poem concerning the state of mind of each? How do you explain the apparently cordial relationship of the two women?

5. How has the poet prepared us for the ending? Reread the poem with this question in mind. Although Taulbe Barton and Lomey Carter were engaged in deadly combat, the wording of the last two lines suggests a closeness and a sharing which we don't usually associate with enemies. What are your reactions to this suggestion?

THE FORSAKEN

I

Once in the winter
Out on a lake
In the heart of the northland,
Far from the Fort
And far from the hunters,   5
A Chippewa woman
With her sick baby,
Crouched in the last hours
Of a great storm.
Frozen and hungry,   10
She fished through the ice
With a line of the twisted
Bark of the cedar,
And a rabbit-bone hook
Polished and barbed;   15
Fished with the bare hook

All through the wild day,
Fished and caught nothing;
While the young chieftain
Tugged at her breasts,   20
Or slept in the lacings
Of the warm *tikanagan*.[1]
All the lake-surface
Streamed with the hissing
Of millions of iceflakes   25
Hurled by the wind;
Behind her the round
Of a lonely island
Roared like a fire
With the voice of the storm   30
In the deeps of the cedars.
Valiant, unshaken,
She took of her own flesh,
Baited the fishhook,
Drew in a gray trout,   35
Drew in his fellows,
Heaped them beside her,
Dead in the snow.
Valiant, unshaken,
She faced the long distance,   40
Wolf-haunted and lonely,
Sure of her goal
And the life of her dear one:
Tramped for two days,
On the third in the morning,   45
Saw the strong bulk
Of the Fort by the river,
Saw the wood-smoke
Hang soft in the spruces,
Heard the keen yelp   50
Of the ravenous huskies

[1] *tikanagan:* an article of clothing that keeps the baby secure at its mother's breast

144

Fighting for whitefish:
Then she had rest.

II

Years and years after,
When she was old and withered,   55
When her son was an old man
And his children filled with vigor,
They came in their northern tour on the verge of winter,
To an island in a lonely lake.
There one night they camped, and on the morrow   60
Gathered their kettles and birch bark,
Their rabbit-skin robes and their mink traps,
Launched their canoes and slunk away through the
    islands,
Left her alone forever,
Without a word of farewell,   65
Because she was old and useless,
Like a paddle broken and warped,
Or a pole that was splintered.
Then, without a sigh,
Valiant, unshaken,   70
She smoothed her dark locks under her kerchief,
Composed her shawl in state,
Then folded her hands ridged with sinews and corded
    with veins,
Folded them across her breasts spent with the
    nourishing of children,
Gazed at the sky past the tops of the cedars,   75
Saw two spangled nights arise out of the twilight,
Saw two days go by filled with the tranquil sunshine,
Saw, without pain, or dread, or even a moment of
    longing:
Then on the third great night there came thronging
    and thronging
Millions of snowflakes out of windless cloud;   80
They covered her close with a beautiful crystal shroud,

Covered her deep and silent.
But in the frost of the dawn,
Up from the life below,
Rose a column of breath   **85**
Through a tiny cleft in the snow,
Fragile, delicately drawn,
Wavering with its own weakness,
In the wilderness a sign of the spirit,
Persisting still in the sight of the sun   **90**
Till day was done.
Then all light was gathered up by the hand of God
    and hid in His breast,
Then there was born a silence deeper than silence,
Then she had rest.

Duncan Campbell Scott

Questions and Comments

1. For what period of time were the mother and son isolated by the storm?

2. What actions demonstrate the mother's resourcefulness and courage in her need to survive? To what extent do you think her concern for her child guided her actions?

3. In certain cultures it is customary for very old people—no longer able to contribute to survival—to leave the community for a lonely death or to be thrown to predatory beasts. Consequently, we can read the abandonment of the old Chippewa woman as a traditional tribal ritual. Discuss how the woman's final sacrifice is related to her using part of her flesh as bait during the earlier ordeal.

4. In the second part of the poem note the "valient, unshaken" echo from the first part. What other images or story elements recur? How does the poet characterize the snow in Part I? In Part II?

5. Do you read religious overtones in the description of the woman's death? If so, which images stimulate these?

"OUT, OUT-"

The buzz saw snarled and rattled in the yard
And made dust and dropped stove-length sticks of wood,
Sweet-scented stuff when the breeze drew across it.
And from there those that lifted eyes could count
Five mountain ranges one behind the other   5
Under the sunset far into Vermont.
And the saw snarled and rattled, snarled and rattled,
As it ran light, or had to bear a load.
And nothing happened: day was all but done.
Call it a day, I wish they might have said   10
To please the boy by giving him the half hour
That a boy counts so much when saved from work.
His sister stood beside them in her apron
To tell them "Supper." At the word, the saw,
As if to prove saws knew what supper meant,   15
Leaped out at boy's hand, or seemed to leap—
He must have given the hand. However it was,
Neither refused the meeting. But the hand!
The boy's first outcry was a rueful laugh,
As he swung toward them holding up the hand   20
Half in appeal, but half as if to keep
The life from spilling. Then the boy saw all—
Since he was old enough to know, big boy
Doing a man's work, though a child at heart—
He saw all spoiled. "Don't let him cut my hand off— 25
The doctor when he comes. Don't let him, sister!"
So. But the hand was gone already.
The doctor put him in the dark of ether.
He lay and puffed his lips out with his breath.
And then—the watcher at his pulse took fright.   30
No one believed. They listened at his heart.
Little—less—nothing!—and that ended it.
No more to build on there. And they, since they
Were not the one dead, turned to their affairs.

Robert Frost

147

Questions and Comments

1. What attitude do the words *snarled* and *rattled* convey? In what way do these words foreshadow the trouble ahead? How do they relate to the description of the saw in lines 14-16?

2. What purpose do lines 3-5 serve in the poem?

3. What is the significance of lines 33 and 34? What do these lines reveal about the poet's attitude toward the people surrounding the boy at his death? Toward the fact of death itself?

4. Shakespeare's tragic hero Macbeth, upon the death of his wife, delivers these lines:

> Out, out, brief candle!
> Life's but a walking shadow, a poor player
> That struts and frets his hour upon the stage
> And then is heard no more.

What reason do you think the poet had for using the first two words of the speech as the title of his poem? How is the speech related to the central idea of the poem?

5. Which elements in this poem probably would not be included in a newspaper account of the accident? What poetic value do nese elements have?

from IN MEMORIAM

Dark house, by which once more I stand
   Here in the long unlovely street,
   Doors, where my heart was used to beat
So quickly, waiting for a hand,

A hand that can be clasped no more—   5
   Behold me, for I cannot sleep,
   And like a guilty thing I creep
At earliest morning to the door.

He is not here; but far away
    The noise of life begins again,   10
    And ghastly through the drizzling rain
On the bald street breaks the blank day.

Alfred, Lord Tennyson

Questions and Comments

1. What is the situation which the poem depicts? What do you guess had been the relationship of the speaker to the departed person?

2. What are the feelings of the speaker toward the dead person? Why do these feelings seem to be different from those of the speaker of " "Out—, Out—" "?

3. Does the world seem to reflect the speaker's grief? If so, which words suggest a grieving world?

4. What is the significance of the final stanza? What view of life and death is reflected in these final words?

THE BUSTLE IN A HOUSE

The bustle in a house
The morning after death
Is solemnest of industries
Enacted upon earth,—

The sweeping up the heart,
And putting love away
We shall not want to use again
Until eternity.

Emily Dickinson

Questions and Comments

1. What associations do you have with the word *bustle* (line 1)? With the word *industries* (line 3)? Do you feel that *enacted* imparts a special quality to the action that would not be communicated by a phrase such as *carried out?* Explain.

2. The poet's use of *heart* (line 5) and *love* (line 6) turns what might have been a literal statement about housework into a metaphor. Which words might be substituted for *heart* and *love* to keep the statement an ordinary one? What word sounds like *heart* and refers to something that might be swept?

3. What ideas about death are suggested in the last two lines of the poem?

LITTLE ELEGY

FOR A CHILD WHO SKIPPED ROPE

Here lies resting, out of breath,
Out of turns, Elizabeth
Whose quicksilver toes not quite
Cleared the whirring edge of night.

Earth whose circles round us skim
Till they catch the lightest limb,
Shelter now Elizabeth
And for her sake trip up Death.

X. J. Kennedy

Questions and Comments

1. List the words and phrases which incite images of rope-skipping. (Which line does not?) How might "turns" (line 2) be interpreted? What are the elements of the metaphor in lines

3 and 4? To what phase of the swinging rope does "night" (line 4) relate?

2. Comment on the rhythm created by lines 1 and 2.

3. Which word in the poem by its sound suggests rope-skipping?

4. The title, as well as lines 3 and 4, implies that Elizabeth is dead. How then do you explain the speaker's petition of earth that it "trip up Death"? Is it in the nature of a childhood rivalry or an appeal that Elizabeth be revived? Or both?

Buffalo Bill's

Buffalo Bill's
defunct
     who used to
     ride a watersmooth-silver
              stallion
and break onetwothreefourfive pigeonsjustlikethat
                        Jesus

he was a handsome man
             and what i want to know is
how do you like your blueeyed boy   **10**
Mister Death

                 e.e. cummings

Questions and Comments

1. In line 2 how does the choice of "defunct" ("not functioning" or "out of business") characterize the speaker? How do the final two lines round out our impression of the speaker and the speaker's feelings about Buffalo Bill?

2. What effects are accomplished by placing "stallion" and "Jesus" apart from their contexts?

151

3. Are the appearance of the poem on the page and its tone appropriate to its subject matter? Explain your answer.

ELEGY FOR J.F.K.

(NOVEMBER 22, 1963)

Why *then*, why *there*,
Why *thus*, we cry, did he die?
The heavens are silent.

What he was, he was:
What he is fated to become   5
Depends on us.

Remembering his death,
How we choose to live
Will decide its meaning.

When a just man dies,   10
Lamentation and praise,
Sorrow and joy, are one.

W. H. Auden

Questions and Comments

1. Are the questions raised in lines 1 and 2 typical reactions to sudden, violent death?

2. Compare the dramatic situation of this poem with that of "Auto Wreck".

3. Auden's style here incorporates a balance of grammatical elements and a combination of seemingly opposing terms

and ideas. List as many of these as you can.

4. Expand on the idea presented in the final stanza. Is this statement true from your experience?

OZYMANDIAS

I met a traveller from an antique land
Who said: Two vast and trunkless legs of stone
Stand in the desert. Near them, on the sand,
Half sunk, a shattered visage lies, whose frown,
And wrinkled lip, and sneer of cold command,   5
Tell that its sculptor well those passions read
Which yet survive, stamped on these lifeless things,
The hand that mocked them and the heart that fed;
And on the pedestal these words appear:
"My name is Ozymandias, king of kings: 10
Look on my works, ye Mighty, and despair!"
Nothing beside remains. Round the decay
Of that colossal wreck, boundless and bare,
The lone and level sands stretch far away.

Percy Bysshe Shelley

1. How many speakers can you identify in this poem? Why do you suppose the poet had "a traveller from an antique land" speak the major portion of the poem?

2. *Which* in line 7 is clearly the subject of *survive*. To what does *which* refer? In line 8 *hand* stands for one human being; *heart* stands for another. For whom does each of these words stand? To what does *them* in line 8 reler? How might *mocked* best be interpreted?

3. What images in the poem suggest decay?

4. What impression do you get of Ozymandias from the words

153

which appear on the pedestal? These words are particularly ironic. Why? What further irony is achieved by the setting in which the ruined statue appears? In what sense was Ozymandias probably using the word *despair* (line 11)? Our response might be to despair for a different reason. What reason might that be?

5. What do you consider to be the central idea of the poem?

ON THE VANITY OF EARTHLY GREATNESS

The tusks that clashed in mighty brawls
Of mastodons, are billiard balls.

The sword of Charlemagne the Just[1]
Is ferric oxide, known as rust.

The grizzly bear whose potent hug
Was feared by all, is now a rug.

Great Caesar's dead and on the shelf,
And I don't feel so well myself!

Arthur Guiterman

Questions and Comments

1. What do the subjects of all the couplets have in common? How are they related to each other?

2. What is the meaning of the title?

3. This poem expresses in lively couplets an idea very similar to that expressed in "Ozymandias." State the idea and compare the tones of the two poems.

[1] *Charlemagne the Just:* emperor of Western Europe from A.D. 800-814

I GET UP AT DAWN

When your teeth decay you cannot
Grow new ones. When your hair falls
Out you cannot plant it again.
I get up at dawn and look
At myself in the mirror.   5
My face is wrinkled, my hair
Is grey. I am filled with pity
For the years that are gone like
Spilt water. It can't be helped.   10
I take a cup of wine and
Turn to the bookcase once more.
Back through the centuries I
Visit Shun and Yu the Great[1]
And Kue Lung, that famous rowdy.
Across three thousand years I   15
Can still see them plainly.
What does it matter? My flesh,
Like theirs, wears away with time.

Lu Yu

Questions and Comments

1. How are the metaphors posed in lines 1 through 3 suited
   to a poem about aging?

2. What can you guess about the people named in lines 13 and
   14? How is the speaker affected by the recollection of these
   people?

3. Learning to live with the certainty of physical decline and
   death is one of humanity's long-standing challenges. Here
   a Chinese poet shows that love of literature and a lively
   imagination can help one grow old gracefully. What other
   antidotes to gloomy thoughts have you found in this section
   of poems?

[1]*Shun* and *Yu the Great:* legendary kings of China who ruled before
2000 B.C.

Composition

1. Author and playwright Clarence Day writes as follows: "The world of books is the most remarkable creation of man. Nothing else that he builds ever lasts. Monuments fall, civilizations grow old and die out. . . . but in the world of books there are volumes that live on, still as young and fresh as the day they were written . . ." Considering the growing use of other communications media, to what extent do you agree with Day's statement? Might there be other callings in life which guarantee a person similar possibilities of immortality? Explain your reasoning.

2. Write a news story based upon the incident presented in " "Out, Out—." "

3. With reference to "Old Christmas," write a short story describing your idea of the events leading up to the shooting of Carter by Taulbe Barton.

4. Let us imagine that you have been elected to the board of directors of a project to establish a brand new world. Concerning the matter of whether or not the people should have immortality, take a position either favoring or opposing limited life-spans for all, and in a composition develop two or three reasons which might sway the other planners.

5. Compare "Elegy for J. F. K." with the passage from "In Memoriam" by Tennyson in regard to dramatic situation, imagery, and theme.

6. Using two or three poems in this section, show how the poet may use certain sounds or rhythmic patterns to help establish the mood of a poem.

THOUGHT AND IMAGINATION

As we have taken "readings" in the climate of poetry, we have witnessed elements of outer weather and inner weather interacting. These examples of humanity responding to the world tell us what human beings are and can become. It is, in fact, the capacity for thought and imagination which makes us different from other animal beings.

While only a few of us can recognize a poem in an onslaught of dandelions in early May, an encounter with a frightened young animal, or the appearance of people's faces in the subway, those who make poems teach us how we can fulfill ourselves by using our human faculties. We can learn to savor the experiences of our lives. We can use the gift of memory to combine our experiences into a meaningful pattern. As readers of poetry, we can have the fun of sharing a "crystal moment" captured in an arrangement of words—focusing our imagination upon the design of a created event. Having done this, we should see as more instructive and more delightful many actual events in our own lives.

The fifteen poems in this section, appearing without "Questions and Comments," provide an opportunity for you to read independently.

TREE AT MY WINDOW

Tree at my window, window tree,
My sash is lowered when night comes on;
But let there never be curtain drawn
Between you and me.

Vague dream-head lifted out of the ground,   5
And thing next most diffuse to cloud,
Not all your light tongues talking aloud
Could be profound.

But, tree, I have seen you taken and tossed,
And if you have seen me when I slept,   10
You have seen me when I was taken and swept
And all but lost.

That day she put our heads together,
Fate had her imagination about her,
Your head so much concerned with outer,   15
Mine with inner, weather.

Robert Frost

I WANDERED LONELY AS A CLOUD

I wandered lonely as a cloud
That floats on high o'er vales and hills,
When all at once I saw a crowd,
A host of golden daffodils;
Beside the lake, beneath the trees,   5
Fluttering and dancing in the breeze.

Continuous as the stars that shine
And twinkle on the milky way,
They stretched in never-ending line
Along the margin of a bay: 10
Ten thousand saw I at a glance,
Tossing their heads in sprightly dance.

The waves beside them danced; but they
Out-did the sparkling waves in glee:
A poet could not but be gay,   15
In such a jocund company:
I gazed—and gazed—but little thought
What wealth the show to me had brought:

For oft, when on my couch I lie
In vacant or in pensive mood,   20
They flash upon that inward eye
Which is the bliss of solitude;
And then my heart with pleasure fills,
And dances with the daffodils.

William Wordsworth

THE SOLITARY REAPER

Behold her, single in the field,
Yon solitary Highland[1] Lass!
Reaping and singing by herself;
Stop here, or gently pass!
Alone she cuts and binds the grain,   5
And sings a melancholy strain;
O listen! for the Vale[2] profound
Is overflowing with the sound.

---

[1] *Highland:* the Scotch Highlands   [2] *Vale:* valley

No Nightingale did ever chant
More welcome notes to weary bands   10
Of travellers in some shady haunt,
Among Arabian sands;
A voice so thrilling ne'er was heard
In spring-time from the Cuckoo-bird,
Breaking the silence of the seas   15
Among the farthest Hebrides.[1]

Will no one tell me what she sings?—
Perhaps the plantive numbers flow
For old, unhappy, far-off things,
And battles long ago: 20
Or is it some more humble lay,[2]
Familiar matter of to-day?
Some natural sorrow, loss, or pain,
That has been, and may be again?

Whate'er the theme, the maiden sang   25
As if her song could have no ending;
I saw her singing at her work,
And o'er the sickle bending;—
I listened, motionless and still;
And, as I mounted up the hill   30
The music in my heart I bore,
Long after it was heard no more.

William Wordsworth

AFTERNOON ON A HILL

I will be the gladdest thing
   Under the sun!
I will touch a hundred flowers
   And not pick one.

[1] *Hebrides:* a group of islands west of Scotland   [2] *lay:* song

I will look at cliffs and clouds   5
    With quiet eyes,
Watch the wind bow down the grass,
    And the grass rise.

And when lights begin to show
    Up from the town,   10
I will mark which must be mine,
    And then start down!

Edna St. Vincent Millay

A BEAUTIFUL VIEW FROM
THE WRONG PLACE

We are not where we thought; the path
misled us. We meant to be elsewhere; instead
we emerged above the harbor.
It is lovely here, though not
what we expected. Gray shacks squat   5
by the sea. We squint
across dunes in the sea's glitter,
eye-biting water of no color: not blue,
not green but brighter. I taste
saltcracked lips. Thirst is the ocean's gift,   10
like this sudden beautiful view
from the wrong place,
like love's gift.

Helen Chasin

FOR ONCE, THEN, SOMETHING

Others taunt me with having knelt at well-curbs
Always wrong to the light, so never seeing
Deeper down in the well than where the water
Gives me back in a shining surface picture
Me myself in the summer heaven, godlike,   5
Looking out of a wreath of fern and cloud puffs.
Once, when trying with chin against a well-curb,
I discerned, as I thought, beyond the picture,
Through the picture, a something white, uncertain,
Something more of the depths—and then I lost it.   10
Water came to rebuke the too clear water.
One drop fell from a fern, and lo, a ripple
Shook whatever it was lay there at bottom,
Blurred it, blotted it out. What was that whiteness?
Truth? A pebble of quartz? For once, then, something.   15

Robert Frost

MIRROR

I am silver and exact, I have no preconceptions.
Whatever I see I swallow immediately
Just as it is, unmisted by love or dislike.
I am not cruel, only truthful—
The eye of a little god, four-cornered.   5
Most of the time, I meditate on the opposite wall.
It is pink, with speckles. I have looked at it so long
I think it is a part of my heart. But it flickers.
Faces and darkness separate us over and over.

Now I am a lake. A woman bends over me,   10
Searching my reaches for what she really is.
Then she turns to those liars, the candles or the moon.
I see her back, and reflect it faithfully.
She rewards me with tears and an agitation of hands.
I am important to her. She comes and goes.   15
Each morning it is her face that replaces the darkness.
In me she has drowned a young girl, and in me an
    old woman
Rises toward her day after day, like a terrible fish.

Sylvia Plath

THERE'S A CERTAIN SLANT OF LIGHT

There's a certain slant of light,
On winter afternoons,
That oppresses, like the weight
Of cathedral tunes.

Heavenly hurt it gives us;   5
We can find no scar,
But internal difference
Where the meanings are.

None may teach it anything,
'Tis the seal, despair,—   10
An imperial affliction
Sent us of the air.

When it comes, the landscape listens,
Shadows hold their breath;
When it goes, 'tis like the distance   15
On the look of death.

Emily Dickinson

A NOISELESS PATIENT SPIDER

A noiseless patient spider,
I mark'd where on a little promontory it stood isolated,
Mark'd how to explore the vacant vast surrounding,
It launch'd forth filament, filament, filament, out of itself,
Ever unreeling them, ever tirelessly speeding them.   5
And you O my soul where you stand,
Surrounded, detached, in measureless oceans of space,
Ceaselessly musing, venturing, throwing, seeking the spheres
   to connect them,
Till the bridge you will need be form'd, till the ductile
   anchor hold,
Till the gossamer thread you fling catch somewhere, O my
   soul.   10

Walt Whitman

THE HORSE CHESTNUT TREE

Boys in sporadic but tenacious droves
Come with sticks, as certainly as Autumn,
To assault the great horse chestnut tree.

There is a law governs their lawlessness.
Desire is in them for a shining amulet[1]   5
And the best are those that are highest up.

They will not pick them easily from the ground.
With shrill arms they fling to the higher branches,
To hurry the work of nature for their pleasure.

I have seen them trooping down the street   10
Their pockets stuffed with chestnuts shucked, unshucked.
It is only evening keeps them from their wish.

[1]*amulet:* a charm worn around the neck to protect against evil
164

Sometimes I run out in a kind of rage
To chase the boys away: I catch an arm,
Maybe, and laugh to think of being the lawgiver.   15

I was once such a young sprout myself
And fingered in my pocket the prize and trophy.
But still I moralize upon the day

And see that we, outlaws on God's property,
Fling out imagination beyond the skies,   20
Wishing a tangible good from the unknown.

And likewise death will drive us from the scene
With the great flowering world unbroken yet,
Which we held in idea, a little handful.

Richard Eberhart

UPON HEARING
A SYMPHONY OF BEETHOVEN

Sweet sounds, oh, beautiful music, do not cease!
Reject me not into the world again.
With you alone is excellence and peace,
Mankind made plausible, his purpose plain.
Enchanted in your air benign and shrewd,   5
With limbs a-sprawl and empty faces pale,
The spiteful and the stingy and the rude
Sleep like the scullions in the fairy-tale.
This moment is the best the world can give:
The tranquil blossom on the tortured stem.   10
Reject me not, sweet sounds! oh, let me live,
Till Doom espy my towers and scatter them,
A city spell-bound under the aging sun,
Music my rampart, and my only one.

Edna St. Vincent Millay

WHEN I HEARD THE LEARN'D ASTRONOMER

When I heard the learn'd astronomer,
When the proofs, the figures, were ranged in columns before
me,
When I was shown the charts and diagrams, to add, divide,
and measure them,
When I sitting heard the astronomer where he lectured with
much applause in the lecture-room,
How soon unaccountable I became tired and sick,
Till rising and gliding out I wander'd off by myself,
In the mystical moist night-air, and from time to time,
Look'd up in perfect silence at the stars.

Walt Whitman

THEME FOR ENGLISH B

The instructor said,

*Go home and write
a page tonight.
And let that page come out of you—
Then, it will be true.*   5

I wonder if it's that simple?
I am twenty-two, colored, born in Winston-Salem.
I went to school there, then Durham, then here
to this college[1] on the hill above Harlem.
I am the only colored student in my class.   10

---

[1]*this college:* Columbia University which overlooks Harlem, a pre-
dominantly black community in New York City

The steps from the hill lead down into Harlem,
through a park, then I cross St. Nicholas,
Eighth Avenue, Seventh, and I come to the Y,
the Harlem Branch Y, where I take the elevator
up to my room, sit down, and write this page: 15

It's not easy to know what is true for you or me
at twenty-two, my age. But I guess I'm what
I feel and see and hear, Harlem, I hear you:
hear you, hear me—we two—you, me, talk on this page.
(I hear New York, too.) Me—who? 20
Well, I like to eat, sleep, drink, and be in love.
I like to work, read, learn, and understand life.
I like a pipe for a Christmas present,
or records—Bessie,[1] bop,[2] or Bach.
I guess being colored doesn't make me *not* like 25
the same things other folks like who are other races.
So will my page be colored that I write?
Being me, it will not be white.
But it will be
a part of you, instructor. 30
You are white—
yet a part of me, as I am a part of you.
That's American.
Sometimes perhaps you don't want to be a part of me.
Nor do I often want to be a part of you. 35
But we are, that's true!
As I learn from you,
I guess you learn from me—
although you're older—and white—
and somewhat more free. 40

This is my page for English B.

Langston Hughes

[1] *Bessie:* Bessie Smith, a black blues singer of the 1920s
[2] *bop:* a type of jazz

THE WRITER

In her room at the top of the house
Where light breaks, and the windows are tossed with
    linden,
My daughter is writing a story.

I pause in the stairwell, hearing
From her shut door a commotion of typewriter-keys   5
Like a chain hauled over a gunwale.

Young as she is, the stuff
Of her life is a great cargo, and some of it heavy:
I wish her a lucky passage.

But now it is she who pauses,   10
As if to reject my thought and its easy figure.
A stillness greatens, in which

The whole house seems to be thinking,
And then she is at it again with a bunched clamor
Of strokes, and again is silent.   15

I remember the dazed starling
Which was trapped in that very room, two years ago;
How we stole in, lifted a sash

And retreated, not to affright it;
And how for a helpless hour, through the crack of the
    door,   20
We watched the sleek, wild, dark

And iridescent creature
Batter against the brilliance, drop like a glove
To the hard floor, or the desk-top,

And wait then, humped and bloody,   25

For the wits to try it again; and how our spirits
Rose when, suddenly sure,

It lifted off from a chair-back,
Beating a smooth course for the right window
And clearing the sill of the world.   30

It is always a matter, my darling,
Of life or death, as I had forgotten. I wish
What I wished you before, but harder.

Richard Wilbur

Constantly risking absurdity and death

Constantly risking absurdity
                    and death
         whenever he performs
                    above the heads
                         of his audience   5
      the poet like an acrobat
                    climbs on rime
                         to a high wire of his own making
and balancing on eyebeams
                    above a sea of faces   10
         paces his way
                    to the other side of day
      performing entrechats[1]
                    and sleight-of-foot tricks
and other high theatrics   15
                    and all without mistaking
         any thing
                    for what it may not be

[1]*entrechats:* ballet movements in which one leaps up and crosses one's legs
several times in the air

For he's a super realist
                    who must perforce perceive   30
          taut truth
                    before the taking of each stance or step
     in his supposed advance
                         toward that still higher perch
where Beauty stands and waits   35
                    with gravity
                         to start her death-defying leap

And he
          a little charleychaplin[1] man
                         who may or may not catch   40
               her fair eternal form
                    spreadeagled in the empty air
          of existence

Lawrence Ferlinghetti

Composition

1. Write your own "Theme for English B."

2. In reference to "Upon Hearing a Symphony of Beethoven" and "When I Heard the Learn'd Astronomer," where do you go and what do you do when you "get fed up with things"?

3. Select one of the poems in this section and, as a novelist might, transform the raw material of the poem into a passage of prose.

4. One aspect of the poetic mind which is noticeable in these poems is a heightened feeling for resemblances and associations. What has set your thought and imagination going along these lines? Write a composition in which you try to give your reader a fresh view of what may be a familiar experience to him.

[1]*charleychaplin:* like Charlie Chaplin, a film comedian noted for his unexpected acrobatics

5. Emily Dickinson's sensitivity to light is profound. After you have read again her poem on page 163, return to "A Light Exists in Spring" (page 9). Contrast her techniques of presenting discrete visual effects with those of the writers of "Kyoto: March" (page 4), "The Date" (page 64), "Incident of the Coast" (page 123), and "A Beautiful View from the Wrong Place" (page 161)

6. Compare any of the following pairs of poems: "I Wandered Lonely as a Cloud" and "The Solitary Reaper"; "Afternoon on a Hill" and "A Beautiful View from the Wrong Place"; "For Once, Then, Something" and "Mirror"; "A Noiseless Patient Spider" and "The Horse Chestnut Tree"; "Upon Hearing a Symphony by Beethoven" and "When I Heard the Learn'd Astronomer"; "The Writer" and "Constantly risking absurdity and death."

INDEX OF AUTHORS AND TITLES

174